M000073059

"When you realize that it's not in your power to change another person or relationship, but it is in your power to seek God on how to walk through the turmoil of relationships, then it's time for you to read *A Long Way Off*. The honesty in which Kitti writes will leave no reader feeling isolated. She provides a valuable and much-needed perspective on the active art of waiting on the Lord to affect change in your life and the lives of those most important to you—your children."

—Peter and Johnnie Lord

"The most devastating news we have ever received was the day we were called by a man in our church to tell us our son had confided in his daughter that he was using drugs. I never dreamed it could happen to us. This was the "official" beginning of our own prodigal son story. Kitti Murray's book is an arm around our shoulders as we continue to stand in the middle of the road, waiting for our son to come home. She captures the heart of a brokenhearted parent, but she also gives great confidence that our hope is always and ultimately in the grace of God, both for us and our son. We can now rest in confidence that our son is in the hands of a God who loves him more than we do."

—A pastor and wife in Asheville, North Carolina

"As an educator and a parent of grown children, I often find myself wanting to provide a concise but powerful word of encouragement to parents in the midst of the fray. Kitti Murray's transparency has become a source of ammunition as I seek to challenge parents to stand their ground against the enemy. Her writings come from a heart that has been molded in the fire of experience. She is honest, articulate, sensitive, challenging, encouraging, enlightening, funny, and compassionate. God has gifted Mrs. Murray with the ability to fit powerful experiences into concise, moving stories. I highly recommend *A Long Way Off* for all parents. For those with young children, seeds will be sown. For those with children in the midst of struggles, they will gain valuable insight and companionship. For those of us with grown children, we are reminded of what God has taught us and the ministry we can have with hurting parents."

—Jim Vaught, headmaster of Providence Christian Academy, Atlanta, Georgia

A Long Way Off

A Long Way Off

Hope & Healing *for* Parents of Prodigals

KITTI MURRAY

BROADMAN
&HOLMAN
PUBLISHERS

Nashville, Tennessee

Copyright © 2004 by Kitti Murray
All rights reserved
Printed in the United States of America

0-8054-2775-9

Published by Broadman & Holman Publishers
Nashville, Tennessee

Dewey Decimal Classification: 306.874
Subject Heading: PARENT AND CHILD \ TEENGERS—
ATTITUDES—JUVENILE

Scripture quotations are taken from the following versions: HCSB,
Holman Christian Standard Bible Copyright © 1999, 2000, 2002,
2004 by Holman Bible Publishers. Used by permission. NIV, New
Inernational Version, copyright © 1973, 1978, 1984 by
International Bible Society. NASB, New American Standard
Bible, © the Lockman Foundation, 1960, 1962, 1963, 1968, 1971,
1972, 1973, 1975, 1977, 1995, used by permission. TLB, The
Living Bible, copyright © Tyndale House Publishers, Wheaton, Ill.,
1971, used by permission. *The Message*, the New Testament in
Contemporary English, © 1993 by Eugene H. Peterson, published
by NavPress, Colorado Springs, Colo. NKJV, New King James
Version, copyright © 1979, 1980, 1982, Thomas Nelson, Inc.,
Publishers. NLT, New Living Translation, copyright © 1996. Used
by permission of Tyndale House Publishers, Inc., Wheaton, Illinois
60189. All rights reserved. KJV, King James Version.

"I Like It, I Love It" used by permission.
Words and Music by Steve Dukes, Markus Anthony Hall and Jeb
Anderson. Copyright © 1995 Dream Works Songs (ASCAP), EMI
Full Keel Music (ASCAP), Lehsem Music, LLC (ASCAP) and
Publishing Two's Music (ASCAP). Worldwide Rights of Dream
Works Songs Administered by Cherry Lane Music Publishing
Company, Inc. Rights for Lehsem Music, LLC and Publishing
Two's Music Administered by Music & Media International, Inc.
International Copyright Secured. All Rights Reserved.

1 2 3 4 5 6 7 8 9 10 10 09 08 07 06 05 04

This book is written
for parents,
but it is dedicated
to
the men in my life:
Bill, Matt, David, Stephen, and Andrew

"There is hope for your future,"
declares the Lord,
"And your children will return
to their own territory."
Jeremiah 31:17 (NASB)

Contents

Acknowledgments

There is a lot I don't know, and there is really a lot I don't know about writing books. For instance, I never knew that when a book is finished, the writer has such a weight of gratitude to get off of his or her chest that an acknowledgements page is nowhere near a mere formality; it is a barely contained tome in itself. So many people, from friends to strangers, helped me along the way.

I must begin by acknowledging a long friendship between two men, without whom I would have written a few more school newsletter articles and called it a day. My wonderful dad and his friend and mine, Steve Bond, had better dreams for me than I had for myself. Thanks. Mom, as always, you provide insight and inspiration. I want to grow up to be just like you. Beth and Joe, *you* are the perfect ones! Thank you for your intelligent encouragement. You help define "loving family" for me. Mom and Dad Murray, you did more than give me Bill, you gave me your unconditional love as well. Thank you.

Julie, Katie, and Margaret, thank you for providing a spiritual scaffolding for my heart. Melinda and Regina, your godly encouragement is foundational to my soul. Several friends and acquaintances read the seedlings of this book in order to give me courage to write more. Mal and Wanda McSwain, Jim Vaught, Steve and Ann Harris, Sandy Case, Marilyn Clemmons, Cheral Turnipseed, Judy Lassiter, and Sue Burton, thanks for wading with me into a daunting undertaking and assuring me that I could swim. John Vawter, thanks for taking time from your own writing schedule to help me with mine. Mary Ann Cuenin, thanks for the peaceful place to write— what a gift. To our family at West Merritts, thank you for your constant grace. I love being a pastor's wife when you are in the equation. To our extended family at Providence Christian Academy, you are a vital part of God's "lesson aims" for my life!

Thanks to Len Goss for walking me through this process from start to finish, for acting like a thoughtful peer, when I was expecting a demanding professor. We've named our driveway after you. To John Thompson, thanks for the crash course in both business savvy and spiritual sensitivity. It is a rare man who practices both.

I suppose if one writes a book, one craves an audience. When it comes to our sons, fine young men all, I hope the house is filled to capacity to hear this: Although I have written about sorrow for others' sake, I could have written reams more about the joy you give me every single day. Thanks for giving your permission for me to expose myself in print. Even though this book is not about you, I have probably embarrassed you, and you take it like the men you are. I love you guys.

When my heart sings with gratitude, the clearest, deepest notes belong to Bill. I'm awed that God lets me be with you in both the rigor and the respite of life. You lighten the former and enliven the latter. To thank you for reading till your eyes crossed, often night after night when your day was already sated with print, is merely to highlight a sacrificial love that you deliver to my doorstep every day. You make grace real.

Finally, to the Lord Jesus Christ, whose sacrifice brings us from a long way off to the welcoming arms of the Father, all praise and glory and honor, forever and ever. Amen.

Introduction

In 1633, two years after John Donne's death, the first volume of his poetry was published. The printer introduced his poems with a note, not to the readers in general, but "To the Understanders." The written word in this volume in no way parallels the poetic genius of John Donne, but it *is* written to a select group of "understanders."

You know who you are. Your circumstances may vary considerably. The child whose life caused you to pick up this book may be thirteen or thirty. Some of you raised your children in what cannot be labeled anything but a decidedly Christian home. Others of you came late to know Christ in your hearts and your homes.

Either way, you love your children. You love them, and in some way or another, that love has hurt you. Your son or daughter did not choose drugs, sexual promiscuity, agnosticism, atheism, or even prison just to hurt you. He did not quit going to church to spite you, and she didn't marry an unbeliever to purposefully distress you. His depression or bipolar disorder or ADD is not a weapon meant to harm you. Her eating disorder is not maliciously calculated to make you anxious or afraid. No, the heartache you experience can be laid at the feet of your love. Young adults everywhere are making these choices and, while it may depress or irritate or anger you, their lifestyles do not make you weep with deep sorrow. But your wayward children do. These pages are addressed, not to the problems in your home, not to the mistakes you may have made, not to your sons or daughters; they are spoken to parents' hearts that have been broken by love.

I so wanted to write a book titled *How to Have a Perfect Family like Mine*; but you will quickly discover that my husband Bill and I are disqualified for such a task. But I can, from this dark side of the parenting planet, offer a consoling pat on the back and a "there,

there" to souls whose hurts I understand. And perhaps, because we understand each other, I have your permission to challenge you to bring the truth of God to bear upon your hurt. That quest—to know God, to believe him, to see our families as he does, to deal with regrets and discover reasons, to regain hope and even joy—is one I invite you to pursue as you read.

CHAPTER ONE
Our Story

O h Lord, I didn't know being a parent would hurt so much!" It
was less a whine than a bewildered moan. Our house was
uncharacteristically still that morning. I was settled on the den sofa
fretting out loud to God (I'm not sure I would call it prayer) over our
oldest son Matt. I remember the exact words and tone of my cry that
day, not because it was sparked by a specific event but because it represented a turning point. At the risk of overdramatizing, I would call
that moment a portent of things to come.

I would not have labeled our oldest son "rebellious" or a "problem child." But the seismic shift from sweet and pliable to sullen
and unreachable had begun. We had prepared for it, read about it,
and talked about it, but our hearts really were not ready. Our
youngest son is there now, on the cusp of all those swirling hormones
and half-formed independent ideas, that frightening omniscience
teenagers have. I *am* ready now. But back then—back when all
I knew about my children was how to charm them into a better
mood, how to reason with them, how to punish them in a straightforward way—I reacted with all the inner terror of a woman faced
with a howling werewolf who just transformed before her very eyes!
The full moon of adolescence was out, and I was caught unaware.

I would like to say that we rode out those years with graceful
parental aplomb. But that isn't the case. In the next few years my
husband Bill and I would watch our oldest son move further and further away from us—our values, our protection, and even our love.
What began as normal teenage changes gradually became hostility,
depression, and eventually drug use. The distance between us wasn't
wedged there overnight, nor did we watch it grow without many
attempts to close the gap. Bill and I agree that the two years or so in

which we both knew "something was wrong" but couldn't identify exactly what it was were the most difficult. Much of the difficulty was that Matt was a teenager, and normal teenagers can be hostile, detached, and perhaps even lawbreaking at times. We found ourselves citing events—an outburst, petty vandalism, friends of Matt's we didn't trust—to older parents, and they would say, "That's normal teenage stuff." But it wasn't.

The Fellowship of Suffering Parents

When we were engaged, my husband had cancer and, fifteen years later, a heart attack at the young age of thirty-eight. Those were hard times, but we both believe that the night we discovered Matt was using drugs produced in us a deeper heartache than either Bill's cancer or his heart attack. Why? First, Matt is our son. If you are a parent you understand. Second, Matt's drug use was his *choice*. In some ways it was like the pain of a divorce when a husband or wife is still desperately in love with and committed to the other, yet the other *chooses* to leave. Finally, it represented a deep hurt inside of him that we felt powerless to touch or heal. Our family has called the years that followed some of our best and worst all in one. We discovered the truth in C. H. Spurgeon's words: "The Lord's mercy often rides to the door of your heart on the black horse of affliction." Matt did begin to heal, and we all did with him. But the process has not been easy or quick.

The fact that we are now card-carrying members of the Hurting Parents Club has given us countless opportunities to talk with other hurting parents. As we have listened to them, we've discovered many who feel that their sense of failure and isolation is often heightened in the Christian environment where everyone else seems to be "doing it right" and getting "right" results. They may not be dealing with major rebellion in their child, but the teenage or young-adult years have thrown them for a loop, and they are reeling.

One day I sat on a bench at a park with a mother whose second grader was in our second grader's class. In the course of the conversation, I shared honestly about our experience with Matt. Tears began to stream down her face. Her son was in a drug-recovery program for the second time, and she assumed no one at our pristine

Christian school could possibly relate. She felt like a pariah. She was aching and alone. As our innocent second graders played that day, we shared a bond that I have since shared with many other parents. It is the fellowship of the hurting, the bewildered, and the sometimes cynical.

I have a page in my prayer notebook with a list, and the children of these parents are on that list. Some are openly rebellious, some have abandoned their faith, some are lost in the haze of drugs, for some sexual promiscuity has left them damaged, and some have not called home in ages. There are also some on my list whose faith is intact and whose relationship with their parents is strong, but they are battling the quieter demons of mental illnesses, eating disorders, or problems at school. This book is for the parents of the young men and women on my list. And for the parents whose children are on someone else's list. It is an effort to wring every ounce of good out of our own experiences, to parlay our pain into a higher purpose.

I might add this plea: if you cannot classify yourself as an "understander," if you have not experienced in at least some small way this sort of parental pain, please close the book, put it down, and back away! My first reason for such a prohibition is purely self-protective. I fear that you, the noninitiate, would be either too quick to judge or too slow to understand. It has been one of the riskiest ventures of my life to write these words, so much so that I tremble to think of them falling into the wrong hands. But my warning is for your own good as well. Young couples would do well to educate themselves about the realities of the life ahead of them as parents; but it would be foolhardy for them to learn about parenting by spending a week cooped up in a home with someone else's colicky infant, two toddlers, and a five-year-old. It would be like going from basic training to the raging battlefront all in one day. Too much exposure too soon could result in either cowardice or cynicism or both. But if you are determined to read on, brace yourself. The truths herein, I am convinced, are sound, but they are hard earned.

"You Are Here"

My hope is that a mom or dad will read these pages and sigh, "I'm not the only one!" Isn't that the first step of comfort? Some of the chapters are more instructional in nature but not instruction in how to raise children. There are many good books on the subject, and I recommend reading a lot of them. These words are for those who, having read the books and made sincere attempts to implement the good advice in them, find themselves feeling cheated by the formulas because, for now, they don't appear to be working. The focus in these pages is not on our children but on us, our broken hearts in need of God's touch. The instruction is from a "you are here" place on the map. How do I think about myself, my children, and God himself during this pain? How do I cope? And, finally, is there hope?

Perhaps the best window into the heart of the pages to follow is to revisit my den sofa. If not from any other place, these words spring from my own sense of failure, loss of faith, and massive amounts of maternal angst. That day, as I cried out to God, I could not help but visit the cross to look into the face of his Son. There I saw a mirror of my own pain. There I heard this challenge: if I am to love as deeply as my Father loves, I will surely hurt as deeply. Raising teenagers and parenting young adults, even without the tragic intrusion of our toxic culture into their lives, can produce in parents a roller coaster of emotions, many of which take up daily combat against our own faith and values. The process of healing as a parent can take place only in the fellowship of Jesus Christ. If we do not find a place to cry out to God, to become intimately acquainted with him in the midst of such a battle, we will be no match for the days ahead.

QUESTIONS FOR REFLECTION

1. What is your "you are here" place on the map?
2. What has been most difficult about that place?
3. Have you already gained comfort by saying, "I'm not the only one?"

CHAPTER TWO

The Courage
of Children

When it comes to climbing, feats of balance and skill, physical pain, jumping, or anything that requires superhuman speed, I am cautious by nature. In other words, I am a coward. By contrast our children were born hurtling, flying, bounding, and rolling with reckless abandon through life. Sometimes I feel like Evel Knievel's mom must have felt. Every time I attempt to join the athletic fray, I am forced to return to my cautious ways. Once I jumped down five steps of our staircase with a running leap, the way the boys did. I forgot to calculate my jump based on my extra foot or so of height. The bruise on my forehead from the solid oak door lintel was embarrassing. Or did you know that, when hit by a twelve-year-old, the speed and trajectory of a whiffle ball can cause it to hit one's face in such a way that one's speech is slurred for two days? *Dis I dnow from experience.*

One day I dragged home, bleeding from a tumble I took during a run. I felt like Iron Woman because I had continued my run, blood on each knee and elbow notwithstanding. The alternative was to limp home and crawl in bed, only to crawl out later stiffer than a two-by-four. I thought my scrapes would rank in my boys' eyes as badges of honor, but I forgot that scrapes and bruises are daily wear for them. All I did as I triumphantly showed them my wounds was confirm the fact that I am a klutz.

Our bravely boisterous sons are truly an inspiration to me, but not because they appear almost leprous with the evidence of countless collisions on their bodies. They inspire me because, knowing they will inevitably acquire those bumps and bruises, they skate, slide, and soar off into the sunset anyway. That is the kernel of courage: knowing the risks and taking them anyway.

Realism

Another kind of courage is distinctly grown-up in nature. It is the courage required to face perils far more serious than a skateboard ramp or a ski slope full of moguls. It is the valor of honesty. It takes nerve to look a problem squarely in the face, especially when the face bears your own image.

I wasn't ready to hazard this sort of honesty on the day we received a phone call from the doctor who admitted Matt to the hospital. Thirty minutes of observation had convinced him that Matt was clinically depressed. I latched onto that word *clinically*. That antiseptic word made the strife we had suffered through in our home much easier to bear. We had isolated a virus that could be treated and then, we hoped, forgotten. The doctor's diagnosis divested the situation of any humanness. I could deal with a disease more easily than a hurting son, a heart-stricken husband, or a wound in my own soul. I wanted a cure, not culpability. And I wanted it all to be over. I wanted a return to our idyllic family life. I wanted to close my ears and sing a childish "la, la, la," song. No song was loud enough to drown out the pain we felt, but this would serve. It was a pat answer that allowed me to postpone being honest.

Our son was still in the hospital when Sunday rolled—not *around* but *over*—me. I was a pastor's wife with the buoyant personality whose life everyone wanted to emulate. We had not been in this particular church quite a year. I wasn't sure I could "do" church that day. Why? I'm sure raw heartache would be reason enough, but I was also reluctant to go public with that heartache. I knew I didn't have the fortitude to hold up the "life will be OK" mask. Life wasn't OK, but I wasn't sure if it was permissible to admit that in church.

George MacDonald writes:

> It is when we are most aware of the factitude of things that we are most aware of our need of God, and most able to trust in Him. . . . The recognition of inexorable reality in any shape, or kind, or way, tends to rouse the soul to the yet more real, to

its relations with higher and deeper existence. It is not the hys-
terical alone for whom the great dash of cold water is good. All
who dream life instead of living it, require some similar shock.[1]

The church can easily become a collection of such dreamers. We become addicted to our notions of what we think life *should* be and refuse to face it as it sometimes is. We are too nice to venture into the realms of "the yet more real." Why is that? I can only answer for myself. I avoid honesty about the dark places in my life because I am afraid. I am even more afraid when that darkness looms over my family. What am I afraid of?

I am afraid I might look bad to others.

I am afraid God might even look bad. I find myself asking him, "How on earth can *this* glorify you?"

I am afraid I'll lose my effectiveness, my voice, as a leader.

I am afraid I'll become a whiner. I don't want to be one of those.

I am afraid I'll hurt and hurt and hurt and never stop hurting. Better to shush it.

These fears leave me loath to risk honesty. Many of us prefer to "dream" life rather than live a real life in our homes or in the body of Christ. We circumvent the healing process by covering the wound. In order to preserve our dream, we refuse to acknowledge our sons' or daughters' problems altogether. I have witnessed again and again parents who live in blissful denial of their child's rebellion; it takes a stout heart to see it.

Or it could be that we see the problem but are unable to endure the pain of the truth, and so we spiral downward in an abyss of hurt, despair, and, eventually, cynicism. I have seen these parents give up on a child in the guise of letting go. This is often a desperate ploy to let go of the pain, but it doesn't work. Once again, facing the facts about our child is not a task for the fainthearted. Surely I have slipped into these versions of cowardice myself.

One of the Courageous Ones

Two friends and I met for lunch one day. Our birthdays fall near each other on the calendar, which provides an excellent excuse for a yearly lunch date. As I approached my friends from the parking lot,

I noticed that one of them wore an expression that belied the occasion. Over lunch she spilled what was written all over her face. She had heard that morning from a niece that her son was smoking pot. It was his senior year, and he is her baby. She was stunned, shell-shocked. And she was not certain the information was accurate. How do you confront your child with a rumor? How do you respond at all to a, "I heard from a friend who heard from a friend" message? We spent our lunch hashing over all the possible ways she could approach the dilemma and came up with nothing. When we respond to rumors, we are a lot like Don Quixote tilting windmills; our enemy is an illusion, and we seem a bit foolish chasing it down.

Finally, we prayed that the truth would come to light, that my friend and her husband would have more to grasp than gossip, or that they would discover the rumor to be nothing more than a wisp of thin air. Several months later, three weeks before their son's high-school graduation, the truth did come to light. But it wasn't light; it was darkness. He and several friends were caught red-handed at school. Not only was his drug use uncovered; he was not allowed to graduate.

My friend walked straight through that darkness with grace from the Lord, grateful for the warning the Lord provided. She and her husband took stock of the situation and faced it with clear eyes. They didn't blame the school or their son's friends. They didn't gloss over the consequences. It hurt, but they faced the hurt. My friend is one of the courageous ones. Finding hope and healing in the midst of pain, especially any pain involving our children, is a daunting task. It is a journey few are brave enough to face.

A Theme Song

The focus of the pages to follow is on the process that ensues in a parent's heart *after* the reality of a child's rebellion or struggle sinks in. Perhaps you have discovered something about your son or daughter that has been a great dash of cold water to your soul. Or you may be languishing in the throes of a long, hard ordeal with your child. He may be a young adult whose life is directionless or, worse yet, patently going the wrong direction. She may be at home, hidden behind a façade of hostility and hardness. You are weary but willing to see the situation as it is. As you have already discovered, these chapters end with probing questions that would best be considered when you have time to deal honestly with them. You may want to use the questions in the quiet and safety of your personal time alone with God. Or you may read and discuss with a few friends who are in the same boat on the same rocky seas. However you do it, if you choose to take your feelings of failure, hurt, frustration, and sheer agony to the Lord for direction and healing, I have a theme song for you.

In the book of Judges, the prophetess Deborah sang a rousing chorus to the people of God that has the spiritual punch of a high-school fight song. Her song was dedicated to the rulers of Israel and chronicled a battle in which the underdogs finally won the day. The lyrics of her song made clear in the beginning that the battle she and God's people fought was the direct result of their sin, specifically the sin of idolatry. Verse 8 of chapter 5 says, "When they chose new gods, war came to the city gates" (NIV). I think it would not be stretching the truth to say that the battle for our children is fought over this same issue. When they choose to live their lives subject to any god less than the true God, eventually war of some sort will visit our gates.

Deborah first painted a picture of a destitute people who longed for restoration. Acting as a deliverer appointed by God, she roused the beleaguered nation for battle. Verse 15 says, "There was much searching of heart" (NIV), as the various tribes decided whether to fight. Not all the people chose to join the battle. In their commitment to maintaining the status quo, several groups stayed behind. For several stanzas Deborah scolded those who, in fear, chose to "stay among the campfires" or "linger by the ships" (vv. 16–17 NIV).

She then turned her attention to those who did fight, who "risked their very lives" (v. 18 NIV). To those brave warriors she intoned, "From the heavens the stars fought" (v. 20 NIV), thus assuring them that God's full resources were available to them for the battle. Her song is a recitation of "the righteous acts of the LORD, the righteous acts of his warriors" (v. 10 NIV). In the last verse of her song in chapter 5, she uttered a blessing over those who were brave in battle: "But may they who love you be like the sun when it rises in its strength" (v. 31 NIV).

I picture this scene like a victory parade on D-day, replete with ticker tape and speeches by the conquering generals. There is one little phrase in Deborah's song that has stayed with my heart as I have faced hard truths and sought God's direction and healing in the face of them. In verse 21, as if speaking to herself, she sang out, "March on, my soul; be strong!" (NIV). As you march through your own process of healing, seeking to love your children honestly and seeking God mightily, may he strengthen your soul for the journey ahead.

And may you have the courage not only to face the realities of your family's hurt within your own heart and before God, but to bravely disclose the truth to at least a friend or two within the body of Christ. You may be surprised at the reaction. That first Sunday of utter vulnerability, when I finally mustered up the courage to go to church, I said to a friend, "We haven't even been here long, and we are already a liability. We are needy and have nothing to offer."

To which she replied, "Now you are one of us. I like you better that way."

QUESTIONS FOR REFLECTION

1. How has the situation you are dealing with at home or in your relationship with a son or daughter required courage?
2. Why do you think it is difficult to face the facts about our families or our children?
3. Who are the friends you can trust to share with honestly?
4. How can you assimilate the message of, "March on, my soul; be strong!" (Judg. 5:21 NIV) into your life?

CHAPTER THREE
Dessert-Cart Choices

Sometimes life is exactly like dessert in a fine restaurant. Just as you are full and satisfied, having been fed and pampered by a conscientious server, up rolls the dessert cart. No less than five delectable desserts dare you from their doilies to find room in your happy stomach for at least one of them. Unless there are five of you at the table and unless you are still comfortable enough for an entire dessert each, you will have to make a choice. Your server patiently turns the cart so that each temptation can call your name. The pastry chef has given them dramatic names like Death by Chocolate or nostalgic names like Apple Pandowdy, so that you feel like you know them and will certainly insult the ones you don't choose. You realize you need a cup of decaf, and it just won't do to drink it without crème brûlée or tiramisu to keep it company. The decision to give in has been made, but which one do you choose?

When life is full of dessert-like choices, the agony is sweet indeed. Do we vacation at the beach or the mountains? Do we buy this car or that SUV? Which color do we paint the house? Which movie do we see? Or even the more significant options: Which church? Which Bible study? Which ministry? It seems a shame to waste any worry over these choices, but we do worry. We are afraid we may miss something better than the good we've chosen.

But what happens if we don't like any of the choices?

On a Thursday night in February, we discovered that Matt had a drug problem. On Friday we began our search for help. Every professional we consulted said the same thing: get him into a drug rehab program right away. But not one of them would write out a prescription in comforting doctor's scrawl with the precise plan on it. We were told what to do but not where or how to do it. So we began a search. Within a week we had a short list of choices. They ranged from wilderness programs that lasted up to two years to outpatient programs that lasted three to six months but would allow him to stay at home. I detested every single option. This was *not* a dessert-cart choice.

Corporate Wisdom

We had done our homework, but we were stuck. We knew we would be wasting valuable time if we didn't act quickly, but no matter how often we stirred the soup, it still looked muddy. It was like choosing the weapon for our own execution. I can't remember whose suggestion it was or how it came about, but one night the next week we invited about twelve friends over for prayer. It was a ploy devised out of desperation, but in hindsight it was pure genius. These friends were not necessarily all our best friends or people who knew each other, but they shared several common denominators. First, they each knew and loved Matt. Second, all but one of them were our age or older and had raised older children. Third, they knew God intimately. And, fourth, they knew how to pray.

They each arrived at our house in quiet determination. Unlike most occasions in our home, we didn't offer them a thing to eat or drink. We just opened our door and ushered them in. Here's how I remember the evening:

We sat in our living room as Bill and I shared as succinctly as we could the options we had. We tried to list them without placing emphasis on any particular plan. That was easy considering how distasteful each and every choice was to us. They asked a few questions, gave a little bit of input, and then we began to pray. I think we just "fell" into prayer. We prayed a long time. You know how group prayer can seem long at times, a bit forced. There was none of that here. It seems to me we never exactly said "Amen." We just looked up when we had exhausted every cry we had to the Lord, and we all knew the answer. We didn't take a vote, but it was unanimous. One of the outpatient programs was the obvious choice. I didn't feel the euphoria I sometimes feel when God gives such clarity, but I was at peace. We all were.

The next day Bill and I informed Matt of our decision. Until that point he had expressed open hostility at the mere suggestion of a rehab program. But we simply mapped out the plan and he accepted it. That very night Bill took him to a meeting of the group he would be joining. He embraced the program and the kids in it immediately. Matt spent the next four months in that program and then another year attending small support meetings within the same group. He gradually began going to AA meetings. For him, at that time, it was effective. It was an answer to prayer.

Because we followed a course we discovered in the presence of many witnesses, the months that followed were easier. The program we chose was not without its problems. Sometimes we felt it was almost cultlike in its control of Matt's time: he was told precisely how to spend his time and with whom. The counselors were all young, and we weren't certain the influence they had over him was always the best. We had to fight to maintain our own standards as his parents. We didn't always connect with the other parents, many of whom were former addicts themselves. Often when we went to bed, riddled with doubt about the choice we had made, we would recall that evening of prayer. We took comfort from knowing we hadn't made the choice in a vacuum.

Recycling Comfort

I have a friend whose husband is battling cancer. She and her husband have a vast network of family and friends in our city, so I have not wanted to call or drop by too often. I have assumed her every need is more than adequately met. One day she called to ask me to come by and pray with her. Believe me, I do not have a rep-utation as a prayer warrior, but I love my friend, and I know what it means to be desperate before God. I know what it feels like to watch your husband stare cancer in the face. She knows that, so she called. I had been praying that God would reveal to me the best way to minister to her. I thought God would send some sort of super-natural impression to my heart, but what could be clearer than a phone call from her with a specific request? I'm so glad she spelled it out for me.

In one sense, every time I have the honor to pray with a friend, I am recycling the comfort our friends gave us that fateful week. Paul understood that our pain serves a higher purpose in this way:

> *Blessed be the God and Father of our Lord Jesus Christ, the Father of mercies and the God of all comfort. He comforts us in all our affliction, so that we may be able to comfort those who are in any kind of affliction, through the comfort we ourselves receive from God. For as the sufferings of Christ overflow to us, so our comfort overflows through Christ. If we are afflicted, it is for your comfort and salvation; if we are comforted, it is for your comfort, which is experienced in the endurance of the same sufferings that we suffer.*
> (2 Cor. 1:3–6 HCSB)

At the time it seemed that the only purpose our meeting with our friends had was to give us our answer, but God was multitasking even when we couldn't. He had others in mind who would need us as desperately, when the time came, as we had needed our friends then.

Support for Our Hands

Why do I share this part of our story with you? Is it so that you will follow our example and hold a prayer meeting at your home with twelve people who match our list of requirements? I don't think so. The essence of that episode in our story is this: our fear, our literal shock, and our pain kept us from making the wisest, best decisions for Matt, therefore we needed the support of friends. They weren't mind readers, so we had to call and ask. In God's never-wasteful economy, there were those who had experienced his comfort and were ready to share it with us.

In Exodus 17, the Amalekites attacked the Israelites as they wandered in the desert. Moses literally held up his hands while Joshua and the Israelites fought the Amalekites. Verse 11 tells us, "As long as Moses held up his hands, the Israelites were winning, but whenever he lowered his hands, the Amalekites were winning" (NIV). God could have given Moses supernatural strength to keep his hands in the air. Moses is the man who awed a pharaoh by turning the Nile to blood. His hands held the staff over the Red Sea while God created a path of dry land through its waters. The same staff struck a rock and produced water for the thirsty Israelites to drink. Surely this is a man who could hold his hands in the air for a day. But, instead, we are told, "When Moses' hands grew tired, they took a stone and put it under him and he sat on it. Aaron and Hur held his hands up—one on one side, one on the other—so that his hands remained steady till sunset" (v. 12 NIV).

Like Moses, our arms were becoming weary from the strain of holding a battle up to the Lord. Our friends were clearheaded enough to know we needed someone to pull up a stone for us to sit on. We were in desperate need of a Hur and an Aaron to bolster our arms for the duration of the battle. There was a real possibility of defeat without them.

Use Your Crutches!

One bright, spring day during my college years, I was bounding up the steps of the student center to attend a Bible study. As I breezed by, I stopped to ask a friend if she was coming. I included the cute guy who was lounging on the steps next to her in my invitation. He looked at me and said, "I don't need a crutch like that."

I have never been adept at snappy comebacks. It took me years to think of one for that young man. Now I wouldn't have to think long to remark, "You may not need a crutch, but *I* do!"

Surely I can lean all the weight of care I will ever have on the Lord. He is able to take my weakness and transform it into his strength. But when I am hurting, I discover that what Jean Varnier says is true: "People are longing to rediscover true community. We have had enough of loneliness, independence and competition."

He surely takes my care upon himself when I seek him in solitude, but solitude is not the only place of healing. He also has given me a community that is populated with emissaries of his strength. When I am needy, when I have tough choices to make, or when I am weary, I can call for reinforcements. Friends who can pray for and with me are the crutches I cannot live without. And I am not ashamed to admit it.

QUESTIONS FOR REFLECTION

1. What difficult choices have you had to make in your family? Are some difficult decisions looming in your not-too-distant future?

2. How can you enlist the help of trusted friends in your search for answers?

3. Why is it tough for you to rely on the help and input of others?

4. Can you see ways God is recycling your pain to comfort someone else?

CHAPTER FOUR

The Other Children—
Feeling Neglected?

My sister has cerebral palsy. She is one of the smartest, funniest, most independent, and accomplished women I know. She also tunes into the feelings of others more astutely than most. Several years ago she called me from her home in California with the express purpose of asking me what it was like to grow up with a sibling whose needs required so much extra attention from our parents. She was doing both academic and personal research and became concerned that my life and my brother's had in some way been "disabled" by her disability.

My first response was, of course, to reassure her that I never, ever—neither then nor now—felt robbed of anything. But she persisted, and I dredged up the only clear memory I have of feeling either neglected or jealous of the place her special needs took in our family. During her young years she endured a number of surgeries. To me those were actually times of adventure soured a bit by my vague awareness of how difficult they were for her. We ate out more, I got to "sleep over" at the hospital with her when I was old enough, and there were always interesting people to meet. But one event always left me green-eyed with jealousy. Every hospital stay a few sweet church ladies would show up the first day with a basket of wrapped presents for my sister to open, one for each day that week. I loved seeing what popped out of each mysterious little box. But more than anything I wanted one of those baskets myself, and I never got one. Poor me, no surgeries!

Maintaining Normalcy

The fact that the memory of those baskets was the best I could come up with in answer to her deep probing is testimony to our parents. First, they somehow managed to meet my sister's more pressing physical needs in such a way that it just seemed normal. I never questioned it. And they obviously cared for my brother and me more than adequately. I'm sure it wasn't easy, but they never made us feel shortchanged in any way. But it wasn't as if they compensated; they just parented well.

This example served as an encouragement to me to walk the fine line between overcompensating for my other children during the all-consuming furor of a crisis and ignoring the other children altogether while consumed with something else. When Bill suffered his heart attack, our children were eleven, nine, six, and four. He was whisked away in a helicopter from our small town hospital emergency room to a larger city hospital where he could receive better care. I walked by his stretcher to the helicopter pad and then watched as it lifted off. As you may imagine, this all took place in a fog. I then drove home to check on the boys. Friends appeared out of nowhere. Several took over the care of our children. Someone showed up with a meal. One friend offered to meet our mothers at the airport when they arrived. Two dear friends came ready to ride with me the two hours to the hospital.

I was packing a small bag when a college student from our church arrived offering to do "anything." He had been playing basketball with Bill when the heart attack occurred, and I could tell he was so distraught he needed to be useful. Suddenly I remembered that I had promised six-year-old Stephen I would take him to the store that afternoon to spend his birthday money. The young man jumped at the chance. Stephen still remembers that outing to K-Mart. At the time it would have been so easy to dismiss my promise to Stephen as frivolous. I would have been more than justified in doing so. Several weeks later my mom made a wise comment that made me thankful I didn't. She said, "Adults need to stop everything in the midst of a crisis. But children need for life to go on as usual. It gives them a sense of security." I saw this advice lived out by a friend when his wife died. Just a day or two after the funeral, his twelve-year-old daughter wanted to go to the movies. He was tempted to say no. He certainly wasn't up to it. But he realized that his daughter desperately needed the soothing normalcy of an outing with friends.

Kids are Tough

Another truth about families is that children are much more resilient than we give them credit for. But sometimes the crisis of one child can have a domino effect in our homes. David, our second child, was obviously the closest to Matt and therefore responded more deeply than the others when Matt's world fell apart. He was also old enough to comprehend what was happening. One evening my husband and I sat with him in his room as he showed us a letter Matt had written to him. He sobbed uncontrollably for quite a while. About the time his tears and grief became rather loud, we realized Andrew, our youngest, was standing outside the room. Bill and I both considered whether to talk with Andrew about his brother's behavior. David's wails of grief sounded disturbing to us, so we assumed they had the same effect on Andrew. We met Andrew in the hall, ready to offer a sensitive explanation. He looked up at us, rolled his eyes and muttered, "Man, he sure is annoying." Everything about his comment told us our worries were unfounded. In his world this was just an inconvenient noise. His lack of understanding actually shielded him from issues far too intense and complicated for him to comprehend just yet.

This does not mean our more compliant children won't, at some point in their lives, feel shortchanged or slighted. Consider the "other son" in the parable of the prodigal son. While his younger brother wasted away his inheritance on wine and women, the Scripture tells us that "his older son was in the field" (Luke 15:25 HCSB), where he was supposed to be. This dutiful son could not help but notice the heartsick look of love on his father's face as he watched for the errant son's return from the "distant country." But a closer look into his father's eyes would have reassured him that the love that lived there was large enough for both of them. The Father's heart is unmistakably clear toward *each* of his sons. With one eye on the party in the other

21

room, he assures his older son, "Son, . . . you are always with me, and everything I have is yours" (Luke 15:31 HCSB).

God Is Sovereign

We are not victims of our circumstances, or our slot in the birth order, or the effects of other's behavior. If God is the blessed con-troller of all things, then I can rest in the knowledge that the "all things" in my family are ultimately under his control. The bedrock of this truth has consoled me many times and in many ways. Because of it, I can be sure our children were meant to have us as parents. They were meant to be first, second, third, or fourth. They were meant to have the complex mixture of innate traits that makes them unique. All these things are, in a real sense, fate. And none of us is ill-fated by the predetermined aspects of our lives.

As I look back on my own childhood and what defined it, I see benefits galore. Contrary to my sister's concerns, I feel blessed to have her as my sister, disability and all. Although I would wish for her sake to have her whole, I have been honored to be a part of her life as it is. I'm privileged to have learned at an early age how to push a wheelchair, how to prop open a door, and how to call up indigna-tion when someone I love is treated condescendingly by strangers. Those things have made me who I am.

Not long after that conversation with my sister, I received a mysterious package from her. Inside were seven colorfully wrapped gifts. Each was labeled to be opened one day at a time.

QUESTIONS FOR REFLECTION

1. If you have younger children, in what ways do they need normalcy in your home? How can you provide that for them?
2. How have they exhibited resilience?
3. Are there some areas in your life or your family's life in which you need to reaffirm God's sovereignty?
4. How can you make your heart of love clear to your other children?

I Am a Mother

I am a mother.
I wear two crowns.
One glitters with the light of praise.
I stately stand, my head held high,
"O, thank you, God, for life," I sigh.
My children, in those golden days,
Bejewel my crown.

I am a mother.
I wear two crowns.
One presses wounds into my brow
Till thorns of pain draw blood
And anguished tears that flood,
And I am begging, "How
To cast it down, this crown?"

I am a mother.
I wear two crowns.
And both are meant to lie
At Jesus' feet on heaven's shores.
I dare not keep them anymore.
To grasp at them would be to die.
I cast them down.

I am a mother
Without a crown.
To cast them down was pure delight.
One I had no right to wear,
And one was never mine to bear.
Darkness must give way to light.
He owns my crowns.

CHAPTER FIVE

A Desperate Parent
Drives Home

Oh, Lord, make him behave today," I cried at 7:50 a.m. as
I stealthily slid our van away from school. In a paranoia born
of my own pain I sensed everyone's eyes following me, branding me
as "that boy's mom."

"Lord, may he not say anything inappropriate, may he follow
the rules, respect the teachers. May we not get one of *those* calls
again. May he not mess up today!"

This was a typical day and a typical prayer. Drug use and depression were not even a dim consideration, but fissures were forming,
and I instinctively felt the quake coming. Accordingly, my prayer
life that year was continually spoken from beneath a load of frustration, hurt, and bewilderment.

But today as I prayed, God gently spoke back, asking me a question. "Is that all you want? Do you just want to make it through the
day unscathed by your teenager's rebellion? Do you only dream of
the status quo for him? Do you want protection from embarrassment? Or do you want more?"

I was reminded of the sky-high dreams I had for all my children:
May they be godly young men who long for God, may they be world
changers, and may they follow Jesus and not the world. First Samuel
10:26 describes Saul's friends as "valiant men whose hearts God
had touched" (NIV). I had asked God to make our sons such men.
I had even bravely prayed that they not be good little church boys
but rather passionate men of faith. "Oh, yes, Lord, *that's* my deepest
desire!" I affirmed.

"Then pray that way."

Thus began not an immediate change in our son but a change in *me*. Through God's grace I began to pray for our sons to be fashioned into young men who would be great in stature for God, and that God would get them there in his way and in his time. I dared to pray "whatever the cost" prayers. His way is the best way but not always the easiest way. I have prayed those more difficult prayers, aching all along the way, but becoming increasingly aware of the depth of God's passionate love for us and for our children.

Kicked Out of School

A good friend of mine was waiting to meet with the administration of her son's school to find out if he would be allowed to stay at the school. She and her husband were praying for God to deliver their son from the disgrace of being kicked out of school. The night before their fateful meeting, my friend was handed a verse to read in a prayer meeting. A random reference on an index card held a message of hope for her. She read 2 Chronicles 20:17: "You will not have to fight this battle. Take up your positions; stand firm and see the deliverance the LORD will give you. . . . Go out to face them tomorrow, and the LORD will be with you" (NIV).

God's Word spoke directly to her heart. She and her husband went to their meeting the next day sure their son would be allowed to remain at school. But her hopes for deliverance on the literal "tomorrow" were dashed. Her son was asked to withdraw from the school. As she left the meeting, she was tempted to discard the truth of 2 Chronicles 20. But over time she began to see that "you will not have to fight this battle" meant a whole lot more than she first thought.

Several positive things have happened as a result of that hard chapter in my friend's life. First, she has learned the truth that the battle for her son's life is not hers but rather fully the Lord's. This has given her renewed confidence in praying for her son. Her confidence in herself or her husband to fight for him was waning. The Lord used something outside of their control to remind her exactly where her trust needed to lie. Second, once she discarded her own picture of how things should progress, she began to see God at work. Her perspective limited God to a literal "tomorrow." Like my friend I have often assigned an expiration date to God's promises in my impatience for him to act. Hebrews 4:7 gives a great picture of the timelessness of God's promises: "God keeps renewing the promise and setting the date as today, just as he did in David's psalm, centuries later than the original invitation" (*The Message*). Finally, in the two years that have followed, my friend's son has not only endured, but he has invited a healing process into his life. He has learned and grown and deepened as a result of a difficult trial. Over time he has become a living example of the promise from God for a great deliverance.

"Whatever the Cost" Praying

So often, when I am driving away in fear, when I leave an encounter discouraged, when I return home deflated, I learn how to pray. The early Christians encountered persecution before they even earned the name "Christian." In Acts 4, the Pharisees promised the apostles that they would make their lives miserable if they so much as mentioned the name of Jesus Christ again. The meeting reads eerily like a backroom encounter with the mafiosi. Everything about it was calculated to strike fear in the disciples' hearts. The Pharisees were incredibly gifted at intimidation. Verse 23 tells us that the apostles "went to their own fellowship and reported all" (HCSB). What immediately ensued was a prayer meeting. The believers ended their prayer with, "Now, Lord, consider their threats, and. . . ." Let me interrupt here to insert what I am afraid my own finish might be: "Consider their threats, and protect me from harm. Thwart their efforts to hurt me. May I escape their clutches and live a happy, productive life. Amen."

I confess that this is often the shameful bent of my prayers. Thankfully, our forefathers in the faith prayed this way: "Now, Lord, consider their threats, and grant Your slaves may speak Your message with complete boldness" (v. 29). This was not spiritual posturing. They were not icing their prayers with a sweet layer of "for your glory" that meant nothing. Many of the men and women who prayed for obedient, God-honoring boldness literally lost their lives as martyrs in the decade to follow. They were in effect saying, "Lord, honor yourself in our lives, *whatever the cost*."

In Ezekiel 14:22–23, God gives a commentary on the aftermath of his severe judgment of his people:

Yet there will be some survivors—sons and daughters who will be brought out of it. They will come to you, and when you see their conduct and their actions, you will be consoled regarding the disaster I have brought upon Jerusalem—every disaster I have brought upon it. You will be consoled when you see their conduct and their actions, for you will know that I have done nothing in it without cause, declares the Sovereign LORD. (NIV, author's emphasis)

Of course, we would never, ever pray for disaster of any kind to befall our children. But sometimes their choices create disaster. Perhaps you have watched those disasters. Or perhaps you only fear them. Note that the disaster spoken of in Ezekiel 14 was one endured by the people of God as a direct result of their sin. Sometimes we see the toll a disaster takes on our childrens' lives, not to mention the rest of the family, and we just want out. "This too shall pass" is the only shred of hope to which we can cling. But a narrow escape just for escape's sake is meager consolation.

This passage defines God's idea of disaster survival. His goal for us and our children on the other side of adversity is a reconstruction of our conduct and actions. In other words, the tough times, in his economy, are meant to make a difference in us. This is the focus of our consolation, the eyes of our faith. If God can take the drug use, the promiscuity, the lost months or years, the rebellion, the wounds, the depression, and digression and create this kind of good in my child, then so be it. And—this is much, much harder to say—if he must allow my son or my daughter to sink deeper into darkness in order to bring about a true survival, then so be it.

He Will Not Come to Destroy

When he was four, our son Stephen hurtled down the stairs at a friend's house, only to bang his sweet little forehead on a sharp table edge at the bottom. The friend called Bill at work and me at home, and we all three converged with a bleeding Stephen at the emergency room. I can still see the suspicion of betrayal in Stephen's eyes as we stood by him while the doctor examined the gash on his forehead. Rather than make the wound better, we, the all-powerful parents, were subjecting him to more pain. The nurse ushered Bill and me out of the examining room, explaining that it would better for Stephen not to associate us with the trauma of the stitching. So now we were abandoning him as well. Stephen, like all our boys, has endured his share of splints, stitches, and X-rays. The only scars he bears are the physical ones because he now knows we aren't responsible for them.

The only way we can safely pray "whatever the cost" prayers for our children is with the mature knowledge that God has their best interests at heart. Even when the consequences of a sinful lifestyle bring about tough times, we know God, while he does punish, does not destroy. Listen to him speak in Hosea 11:

> Oh, how can I give you up, Israel? How can I let you go?
> How can I destroy you like Admah and Zebolim? My heart is
> torn within me, and my compassion overflows. No, I will not
> punish you as much as my burning anger tells me to. I will
> not completely destroy Israel, for I am God and not a mere
> mortal. I am the Holy One living among you, and I will not
> come to destroy. (vv. 8–9 NLT)

Morally, spiritually, mentally, emotionally, or even physically, our children may be languishing in a critical care unit because of their own choices or as a consequence of their own sin. We visit them there, but we cannot release them. Our prayers for healing and release are directed to a God who overflows with compassion, even in the midst of his burning anger. He is the Holy One living among us, and we can trust him to do his will in our children, "whatever the cost."

Parenting Power Tools

Does praying for God to have free reign in our sons' or daughters' lives mean we are sitting on our hands? It may feel like it. And there's the rub, because we like to feel useful. I know I do. That must be why I like tools. I like gadgets that are efficient and get the job done—those jar-opening thingies, multipurpose screwdriver/wrench/plier whatchamacallits or simply a good pair of scissors. As parents, we have searched for effective tools—classes, studies, books, and wise counsel. Adolescence surely threw a wrench (sorry!) into the works of our home. It is tempting to head to the parenting Home Depot (wherever that is) and buy a new toolbox. While regrouping and strategizing are wise moves for parents of teenagers and even adult children, it's not wise to throw out the old toolbox. Maybe we need to remember just how powerful the tools we've had all along really are. Praying "whatever the cost" prayers for our children with the Word of God to guide us can be the most effective thing we do as parents. Jeremiah 23:29 says, "'Is not my Word like fire?' declares the LORD, 'and like a hammer that breaks a rock in pieces?'" (NIV). These two power tools, prayer and the Word, are the mighty weapons we wield.

I am certain that nothing I have ever said to my kids is as powerful as the fire or the hammer of God's Word. I read those words, and I can be sure that any of God's Word my children have heard or will ever hear will act as an internal blowtorch or a spiritual sledgehammer in their hearts. So, even if they are not listening now, I can pray:

O Lord, burn purity into their lives.
Crash through the barriers they have erected to you.
Break down the strongholds.
Father, create a fiery passion for you within them.

As I read God's Word and pray the tough prayers—the "burn and break" prayers, the "whatever the cost" prayers—I can rise from my knees with a renewed confidence. In a time when our confidence as effective parents is so often assaulted, it is comforting to know that we carry such powerful tools in our toolbox.

QUESTIONS FOR REFLECTION

1. How do you pray for your child or children when you are desperate?
2. What disasters are you afraid of?
3. What disasters have you and your family experienced?
4. Why is it difficult to pray "whatever the cost" prayers for your children?
5. What needs to be broken or burned away in your own life or the life of your child?

CHAPTER SIX

A Tale of a
Perfect Home

O nce upon a time there was a perfect home. Two perfect children lived there, and these children were loved perfectly by a
perfect Father. Look as you might, you could not find an iota of dys-
function in this home. The words "I'm sorry" were never uttered:
they were unnecessary. The children and the Father communicated
intimately and lovingly and honestly. There was no generation gap.
The children's needs were met. In fact, the Father worked diligently
to provide an entire world for them. Yet while he lavished gifts upon
them, one could never accuse the Father of spoiling his children.

You might think all this perfection was the result of adherence
to a long list of rules. Actually, the contrary was true. The Father
gave his children *one* rule. That's it. A perfect home, perfect provision, perfect parent, and only one rule. It was heaven!

You all know the tragic end of this tale of a perfect home. Alas,
the children chose to disobey their perfect Father. Their one act of
defiance turned their Daddy into a distant figure, a remote Parent
biding his time until another perfect Son could restore him as Dad.
For a while, the perfection was banished. Family and home became
imperfect; communication suffered, providing became difficult, and
"I'm sorry" became necessary words. Work that had been a delight
became a chore. Beauty suffered, order faltered, right wavered.
A fairy tale existence became a much-less-than-perfect reality.

I wonder how quickly the decline from sublime to sordid took
place in Eden. Did Eve detect the difference the first time she had
to clean and scrub the soiled nooks and crannies of her new home?
Did she cry the first time Adam spoke harshly to her in anger or

recoil at the sound of her own voice the first time she nagged or needled him? And how about those sons of theirs? Was their bewilderment as stark as ours can be when Cain and Abel treated each other as siblings often do? As their once-perfect bodies aged and weakened, were they taken aback? We forget that the first family, while as infected with sin as ours, held Eden in their memory banks. Did that make their regret more poignant, more painful?

Haunting the Gate of the Eden

I think we all harbor some sort of glossy, one-dimensional image of the perfect family. To be honest, bad dispositions, crooked teeth, and underachievement don't fit the profile. I'm afraid my perfect-family profile is often influenced far more heavily by the snapshots of families on vacation in the cruise advertisements than by any real sense of what is good and healthy.

A friend came up with a magazine concept called *Realistic Living* which would showcase colorful photos of a typical family playroom littered with toys and half-finished art projects. A twelve-year-old's closet floor might be featured, or the muddy shoes left in disarray on the back porch might grace the cover. I am savvy enough to know her idea would never fly. We all love beauty and order; we all but worship good and right. We love to look at it, dream about it, applaud it, and even hope for it. We have a natural disdain for the opposite. Why else would we save our camera film for when our kids are clean faced and dressed up? Why do we pull out the camcorders for those shining moments of achievement?

But we are also painfully aware of the vast chasm between the perfect images and the real life we experience. Ralph Hodgson's 1917 poem, "Eve," finds Eve waylaid by Satan as she picks berries in Eden. The final stanza mourns:

> *Picture her crying*
> *Outside in the lane,*
> *Eve, with no dish of sweet*
> *Berries and plums to eat,*
> *Haunting the gate of the*
> *Orchard in vain.*

Isn't this a picture of us? Why do we have phrases like, "It's too good to be true" or "I'm just waiting for the other shoe to drop," if we weren't on every level aware that we are *outside* Eden's gates?

What Test?

Have you ever heard the phrase, "The older I get, the better I was?" I think that's the way I remember myself as a student. I remember the As, the few awards, the subjects in which I excelled. And sometimes I totally forget those trying middle-school years. One night our eighth-grade son asked for help studying for a big science test. I quickly learned that *help* meant, "Read the chapters, digest the pertinent facts, and teach it to me." This process began at 9:00 p.m.! I went to bed feeling frustrated that I had done such a poor job teaching my son proper study habits. By the time I fretted myself to sleep, I had become convinced our son would never be prepared for the rigors of life and that I was a miserable failure as a mother.

It was in this mind-set that I greeted the first mom who showed up for our once-a-month eighth-grade moms' prayer meeting the next morning. Before the coffee was poured, she began describing the fiasco of a study time she and her son had the night before. Seems he neglected to take good notes in class, nor did he read those science chapters. She was feeling like, you guessed it, a miserable failure. The doorbell rang, and we ushered in another mom. She politely listened to us continue our complaints, and then a look of horror crept onto her face. "What test?" she exclaimed. At least *our* sons had studied!

They say misery loves company, and I tend to agree. But when those moms left my home two hours later, I was no longer miserable. Why? First, I knew I wasn't alone. These women and their sons were human reminders that eighth graders are still only fourteen and therefore don't possess the study skills of a grad student. And even if I did need some drastic improvements as a mom, I wasn't alone in my deficiencies. Second, what I neglected to do the night before in the midst of my solitary malaise I found the strength to do in the company of friends. I poured out the feelings and frailties (mine and my son's, but mostly mine) to the Lord. The result was a lifting of the load mixed with some therapeutic laughter. What appeared dismal the night before became downright funny by morning light.

The Downward Spiral

I still, especially in those dark, neurotic nighttime hours, rankle that my home, my family, *my life* is not perfect. Something as innocuous as a study session gone awry can set me on the path of selective perception. I begin to view my child in an increasingly negative light, eventually focusing only on the negative clues that support my dreary diagnosis. This is the path to fear. I must admit there have been times when my perceptions have been startlingly astute with nothing selective about them. If I have evidence that one of my children is indeed on a downward spiral into—you name it—drugs, alcohol, sex, dropping out of school, and so on; then I am on the downward spiral too. My fears deepen as I watch what was never perfect become even less so.

In Romans 1, Paul describes the downward spiral of our imperfect world in alarmingly twenty-first-century terms. He portrays a society we have become all too familiar with on our televisions, in our movie theaters, and, for some of us, in our own homes. Not too long ago I read the verses describing "every kind of wickedness" and felt sick to my stomach because I knew my own son was one of those: "proud, and boastful. They are forever inventing new ways of sinning and are disobedient to their parents. They refuse to understand, break their promises, and are heartless and unforgiving" (Rom. 1:30–31 NLT). I couldn't pin every one of those epitaphs on him, but I couldn't escape the resemblance. It was one of those times when God's Word weighed heavily and, for a day, it only added to my fears.

The next day I still had the taste of Romans 1 in my mouth when I opened to Romans 2 and read, "You may be saying, 'What terrible people you have been talking about!' But you are just as bad, and you have no excuse! When you say they are wicked and should be punished, you are condemning yourself, for you do these very same things" (v. 1 NLT). I decided I had better keep reading, and I was quickly reminded that, "No one is good—not even one. No one has real understanding; no one is seeking God. All have turned away from God; all have gone wrong" (Rom. 3:10–12 NLT). And then, just as verse upon verse condemned me, I read the familiar words, "But God proves His own love for us in that while we were still sinners Christ died for us!" (Rom. 5:8 HCSB). So whether I am spiraling downward over some small infraction of my child's that has imbedded in my mind or over the big, obvious sins that threaten to destroy us, the gospel comes to the rescue!

Wait for it Patiently

Why do we expect our own homes to resemble that first perfect one? It is because that was the original plan. Until our own families—we ourselves—are restored to that intended home, we will ache for it. In Romans 8, Paul says:

> For we know that the whole creation has been groaning
> together with labor pains until now. And not only that, but we
> ourselves who have the Spirit as the firstfruits—we also groan
> within ourselves, eagerly waiting for adoption, the redemption
> of our bodies. Now in this hope we were saved, yet hope that is
> seen is not hope, because who hopes for what he sees? But if
> we hope for what we do not see, we eagerly wait for it with
> patience. (vv. 22–25 HCSB)

If our own planet groans, why not our homes? Our families? Our own hearts?

Paul's last sentence mystifies me. "But if we hope for what we do not see, we eagerly wait for it with patience" (HCSB). Somehow patience in the here-and-now is connected to our hope of a new heaven and earth in the future, a restoration of the Eden we've missed. As I think about this in relation to my family, I can offer three personal insights:

First, there is still a life that we do not yet have. Being around others, like my friends with eighth-grade sons, helps remind me that we are each still living an imperfect life. My own experience of failure underscores the truth even more, and the Scripture makes it impossible to ignore. I haven't arrived, and neither have my kids. Glib but true.

Second, there is a personal instruction to wait for "it;" for a new perfected self (like Eve) and a new perfected home (like Eden). When I am taut with frustration at my imperfections that please neither God nor me, I can *know* that the day of redemption is coming. Jeremiah 31:12 promises a day when we "will never languish again" (NASB). So it is with my children. Rather than fret over the next hurdle of change or development I long to see in them, I can reroute my frustration with this thought: *Someday we will arrive at perfection!* It is not a Pollyanna sentiment; it is truth.

Third, knowing that the final outcome is assured makes working toward small goals now a grace-filled prospect. My husband and I recently went on a cruise. Unlike most cruises, all the tipping was included more than adequately in the cost of the trip. I don't have anything to compare it to, but it seems as if the service the staff offered to us was, while excellent, relaxed. They weren't fretting that we might "stiff" them, so they were able to do their jobs well without any anxiety. Like our waiters and cabin stewards, we know our final outcome. It is written in the contract. Thank goodness it is not a payment or tip because we don't deserve either. But God has graciously promised us adoption into his family and the redemption of our bodies to make us suited for our new home.

Until then we can wistfully remember that perfect home. Like Eve, we can peer into our fruit basket, find it empty of paradise's fruit, and, in our sorrow, loiter at Eden's gate. For we know that the day will come when the gates will open and our Daddy will welcome us home.

QUESTIONS FOR REFLECTION

1. What does your perfect family picture look like?
2. What has influenced the forming of that picture?
3. How does the truth that you and your family are not perfect help you to have peace?
4. How does a reminder that the perfection from which Adam and Eve fell will be restored bring hope to you as a parent?

CHAPTER SEVEN
Our Children,
Our Seed

One segment of one molecule of Lisa Harvey Lepovetsky's DNA is three stories high. Not just any molecule, a molecule of mitochondrial DNA, the DNA that is passed only from mothers to daughters. When the science department at Agnes Scott College, my alma mater, designed the atrium of their new $36.5 million science center, they didn't want to grace the blood-red, three-story east wall with just any DNA. They hunted until they found a direct, female, fifth-generation descendant of Agnes Scott herself. The larger-than-life rendering of a microscopic drop of Lisa's blood gives a personal touch to the familiar helix design. In another building on campus, Agnes Scott's staid visage peers out from a heavy, gilded frame. One can almost picture the five generations passing personality traits and physical characteristics from frame to frame.

The idea that children possess a unique mixture of the traits of their ancestors, immediate and ancient, is not new. Over and over, the Scripture calls our children our "seed." Before electron microscopes, it was common knowledge that children are stamped with at least some of their parents' distinctiveness. One of my sons holds his mouth and breathes exactly the same way my dad does when he is concentrating. Another has the same calm, objective way of thinking my husband has. The similarities can be uncanny. The tilt of a head, the style of running or walking, even the predisposition to be chronically early or late. If the biblical metaphor has any real significance (and the Scripture is never flippant in its use of metaphor), it means we reproduce much more than DNA in our kids. We pass on to them an identity, a point of reference, a purpose. A seed from our plant is who they are. Who we are comprises much of their defini-tion and their destiny.

Dormancy

When our children are teenagers, it may seem we picked up the wrong plant at the nursery. The tag says "begonia," but they look and smell like azalea plants. (I was going to write "stinkweed" but decided that wasn't very nice.) Or, to put it even more honestly, there is no evidence of plant life at all! The pot is full of loamy, rich potting soil and a stub of dry, brown growth. We taught them man-ners, work habits, truth, morals; and the lessons have atrophied. But maybe *atrophy* is the wrong word.

If you remember botany class, you know what dormancy is. I think the concept of dormancy aptly reconciles the idea of a nur-tured seed with the wasteland quality of the teenage and young adult years. Early on we watered, fed, fertilized, and sat our promising seeds in the sunny windowsill. We watched and may have been encouraged to see bright green shoots of life, even a blossom or two. There is nothing more lovely than first growth. But winter came, and the plant seemed to wither and die. We despaired and even con-sidered removing the pot to the basement. But, despite appearances, the seed is still alive and well. It may be buried beneath a foot of hard, frozen soil. By the nature of its "seed-ness," it is resting, wait-ing, biding its time until the warmth and rain of spring releases it to its full plant potential, hardier than ever.

I remember the first time our oldest son brought a girl home. It was middle school, she was a cute neighbor friend, and he was smit-ten. For several months we had been bewildered at his surliness and unmannerly habits. So we watched in amazement as he opened the door for her. He awkwardly helped her take her coat off and then, miracle of miracles, hung up her coat in the closet. My husband marveled because he didn't know our son even knew we had a coat closet! This resurrection-by-romance is the stuff of country songs and epic poems. In "I Like it, I Love it" Tim McGraw croons:

> *My mama and daddy tried to teach me courtesy.*
> *But it never sank in 'til that girl got a hold of me.*

Now I'm holding umbrellas and openin' up doors.
I'm taking out the trash and I'm sweepin' my floors.[2]

It's a rather benign example, but it illustrates the concept of dormancy well. The manners were there, buried beneath the hard, rocky soil of adolescence. The fact that a sweet young girl could surface them in him gave us hope that they would emerge in full bloom eventually.

If adolescence alone can create the fallow condition of dormancy, the addition of anger, rebellion, drugs, immoral behavior, or depression can certainly shove the seeds deeper into frozen soil. Our son referred to the process of drug recovery as "getting my conscience back." A teenager with no conscience is a scary sight. The loss of something you may have worked so hard to instill can feel a lot more like death than dormancy. But, as Billy Crystal says in *The Princess Bride*, "He isn't dead. He is only mostly dead." Perhaps it would be helpful to revisit the losses you see in your son or daughter's life and redefine them:

Rejection of authority—dormant submission
Loss of conscience—dormant goodness
Refusal to accept unconditional love—dormant self-esteem
Loss of self-respect—dormant confidence

The DNA of God's Word

If, like me, you have long stretches of doubt, either that you adequately implanted such virtues in your children or that the implants ever took at all, there *is* a seed in your child that promises to bear fruit. It is not your DNA, nor is it the lessons you taught. It is God's Word. Isaiah 55:10–11 describes the following process:

As the rain and the snow come down from heaven, and do not return to it without watering the earth and making it bud and flourish, so that it yields seed for the sower and bread for the eater, so is my word that goes out from my mouth: It will not return to me empty, but will accomplish what I desire and achieve the purpose for which I sent it. (NIV)

You would not be reading this particular book if it was not true that somewhere, in some way, at some time, you delivered the seed of God's Word to your child. He may have twisted it, ignored it, laughed at it, disobeyed it, and trampled upon it since then, but the seed is there and not just the seed. Through Isaiah, God tells us that the elements conducive to the growth of that seed are inherent in the planting of it. The genetic outcome of the DNA of God's Word is predetermined. He says it himself: "It will not return to me empty, but will accomplish what I desire and achieve the purpose for which I sent it" (NIV).

I remember some of the Scripture my boys learned as children. Our oldest memorized Isaiah 53:6 ("All we like sheep have gone astray" KJV) a bit askew. In his best recitation voice, he would say, "All we love sheep. . . ." (We had to remind him that we only *liked* sheep!) It is a comfort to scan over the past years and see not just my own failings but also the indelible presence of God's Word in our family's life. Sometimes in spite of themselves, our children have thoughts, leanings, a way of looking at the world that includes biblical truth. In a chest of drawers in our living room, I have designated drawers filled with my children's old drawings, schoolwork, certificates, and awards. It isn't just sentiment when I find tears springing to my eyes at the sight of a Bible verse written crookedly beneath a scribbled picture. It reminds me of the presence of a living seed within.

I have watered those seeds with tears. Haven't you? Tears of impatience and frustration. Tears of longing for the seed of God's Word to germinate and grow. Tears of joy when there are encouraging signs. Tears of hope. Psalm 126 gives me a picture to look forward to: "Those who sow in tears will reap with songs of joy. He who goes out weeping, carrying seed to sow, will return with songs of joy, carrying sheaves with him" (vv. 5–6 NIV).

I wrote the following little poem for a class of young children to send to their parents. It has the lilt of a small child's voice. It reflects the sweet sentiments of a first grader. You may have forgotten that voice. And the sight of a blossoming plant turned to the sun may be a fading memory. But look and listen. The dormant seed says the same thing. Just not out loud.

QUESTIONS FOR REFLECTION

1. Does *dormancy* describe your son or daughter?
2. Describe what that looks like in his or her life.
3. Think of some of the ways your children have heard the Word of God. How does it comfort you to know they have the seed of the truth in them?
4. What are some of the encouraging signs of life you have seen recently in your son or daughter's life?

Our Children Speak

You are my heritage,
　　I am your future.
You are the rooted plant,
　　I am the seed to nurture.
You make me rich,
　　I make you shine.
You began the race,
　　I am next in line.

You are my depth,
　　I am your brand new layer.
You are my teacher,
　　I am your answered prayer.

CHAPTER EIGHT
Do Something!

It was our first dinner in our first home. Everything we owned was a wedding gift, and I had polished it all until it gleamed. The meal was a painstaking event, especially since we had invited not just one but *eight* couples over for dinner to crowd around our little table and some borrowed card tables. I didn't burn anything—at least not on the second try. I only broke one of the new wedding gifts. (How was I to know a glass dish would break on a hot burner?) Our guests were gathered in anticipation, and I was finally relaxing when my husband bowed his head to say grace.

"Oh Lord," he intoned emphatically, "Bless this food. Do *something* with it! Amen."

He looked up, grinning at his own cleverness. Until he looked at my face. To his credit, he has never prayed over my cooking like that since.

We laugh now at that night and that prayer, but I'm not so sure it was a bad way to pray. Think about it. We work diligently and carefully raising our children. They ask for the proverbial fish, and we know better than to give them a snake. We give them bread, not stones. We start out with shiny new (to us) principles, ideas, and plans. We polish our efforts a bit more when company is around. When our kids are small, we may even pray in mock dismay, rolling our eyes at their silly antics. But at some point many of us find ourselves crying out to God with not a hint of irony, "Do *something*!"

Jesus said it in an almost offhand way, "Even you, being evil, know how to give good gifts to your children" (author's paraphrase). All our preparing, polishing, and posturing has an inevitable strain of evil that begs for *something* to intervene. Underneath the despair of such a prayer is the keen awareness that the *something* must be done by someone far more capable than ourselves. And the something is beyond our paltry abilities; it must be done by the only capable Someone we know.

And Then Something Happened

In Galatians 1, Paul describes his account of his face-to-face encounter with Jesus Christ on the road to Damascus in these words, *"But then something happened!"* (NLT, author's italics). That little phrase in verse 15 houses volumes of truth. Paul's entire life pivots upon that moment. As do ours. We look at the pre-Damascus Paul in the early pages of Acts and see a man in need of a makeover. He is violent, and we wish him to be more peaceful. He is a legalist, and we would like to see grace in him. Where he is cold and harsh, we would rather him be loving and kind. At first blush we might assume that the "something" Paul refers to is his dramatic transition from harsh to kind, from violent to peaceful, from legalist to full of grace. But, and this is a crucial nuance, the *renovation* occurred on the heels of and purely as a result of a *revelation*. Verse 16 identifies the something that we know utterly transformed Paul's life from that point on: "Then he revealed his Son to me" (NLT).

Two of Jesus' followers experienced a similar "something" while walking on a road toward the Jerusalem suburb of Emmaus. What strikes me about this story is the fact that these men spent a good part of their journey with Jesus without knowing who he was. Finally, as Jesus breaks open a loaf of bread, their eyes are opened. "Suddenly, their eyes were opened, and they recognized him" (Luke 24:31 NLT).

As they look back over the encounter, the two men comment to each other, "Weren't our hearts ablaze within us while He was talking with us on the road and explaining the Scriptures to us?" (v. 32). The feeling they experienced was a result of companionship with the risen Jesus on the Emmaus Road.

The Something and the Someone

These phrases in God's Word have provided me with an irreducible minimum prayer for my sons. When I am in such agony that I can barely form words, I can pray for a revelation of Jesus to their hearts. There may be a long laundry list of renovations that need to take place, but I know a face-to-face encounter with Jesus himself is the only real impetus for true renovation. I know that the blinding light of Christ or the subtle strange warming of his presence as he shows up on their road is the best "something" for which I can ask. So the Someone and the something are actually one and the same! I can still pray for my kids: for an improved grade in chemistry; for the right college roommate; for a humble spirit; for the healing of a soccer injury; for godly friends; for a delightful, Christ-honoring spouse; for the right career path. But my list starts with a cry for an appearance in their lives of the One to whom I pray.

In one sense this emphasis in my prayer life has tested what I truly believe about Jesus. It is rather easy to sing solo "You are my all in all," and mean it. For over twenty years I have had a front-row seat to God's all-sufficiency in my own life. But to lay aside the extensive wish list I have for my children and distill it all into a longing for Jesus to become their "all in all" is to affirm that he really is all they need.

I have known three women with sons in prison. Each one of them can sincerely thank God because a prison cell provided the exact environment needed to open their sons' eyes to a revelation of Jesus. Of course each one grieves the loss of some pretty strategic years in her son's life, but a college degree, a prestigious career, or even the hope for grandchildren pale in the light of a son who now knows and follows Jesus Christ. Of course, I have prayed with each for lenient sentencing or early parole, but I have joined these lovers of God in praying that not a minute of the suffering would be lost in God's redemptive plan.

The road your child plants his or her feet upon may, for a time, seem to lead further and further away from Jesus. Psalm 107 gives a detailed rebel's travelogue. You may be able to picture your son or daughter in one of the following scenarios:

Verse 4: "Some wandered in desert wastelands, finding no way to a city where they could settle." (NIV)

Verse 10: "Some sat in darkness and the deepest gloom, prisoners suffering in iron chains." (NIV)

Verse 17: "Some became fools through their rebellious ways and suffered affliction because of their iniquities." (NIV)

Verse 23: "Others went out on the sea in ships." (NIV)

In each case the verses in between chronicle the same repeating pattern. Following rebellion and escape is a period of despair in which all seems lost. In verse 12, the vacuum appears airtight, "So he subjected them to bitter labor; they stumbled, and there was no one to help" (NIV). The consequences of sin in my child's life may mean that he ends up in a place where, "there was no one to help." My mother's heart can barely stand the thought. But then comes the same pivotal phrase, four times in the chapter, "Then they cried out to the Lord in their trouble." Note the condition in which these mutinous ones finally encounter the Lord: "in their trouble." Fast on the heels of the desperate tableau of tribulation is the picture of a rescuing God who can meet our rebellious children with power and forgiveness.

The Lord Will Hold Me Close

By now this idea may be resonating within you.

"Yes, that's what my son needs, a face-to-face encounter with Jesus."

"If only my daughter could meet Jesus on her road, I know she would be OK."

All well and good. But what about you? Is there a "something" that needs to happen in *your* life? Or maybe, in all the events that swirl around the crisis you have experienced with your son or daughter, you have lost sight of your Someone. I don't know about you, but I come back to this over and over again. I am watching my dusty, aching feet as I plod toward the next task, or I have my eyes trained on my new running shoes as I barrel at breakneck speed toward the next destination, and I suddenly realize I am alone. The irreducible minimum I pray for my child is precisely the same I pray for myself. I need a revelation of Jesus. David knew the difference between a road alone and a road blessed with God's presence. "Don't leave me now; don't abandon me, O God of my salvation, even if my father and mother abandon me, the LORD will hold me close" (Ps. 27:9–10 NLT).

Part of the pathos of parenting a teenager is the inevitability that you will be abandoned. Some teenagers separate from their parents with more grace than others, but, to some degree, they all leave home. Many roads lead them away from you. College, career, a spouse, ministry—all bring about separation. You are raising them to leave you. What better road to travel than with Jesus. What loneliness and loss without him. David recognized his Lord and cried, "My heart has heard you say, 'Come and talk with me.' And my heart responds, 'LORD, I am coming'" (Ps. 27:8 NLT).

QUESTIONS FOR REFLECTION

1. What is the "something" that needs to happen in your child's life? Do you have a sense that Christ needs to "show up" on his or her road?
2. How can you summarize your prayers for your child in this way?
3. What is the "something" that needs to happen in your own life? Restoration of hope? Healing? Repentance?
4. How can the presence of Jesus accomplish these things?

No

Depths of darkness
Dank and cold
Hear now my no
Punctuated, italicized,
Underscored, and bold.

No,
You may not have my children,
No,
You may not steal the truth they hold,
No,
You may not mock the light in their hearing,
Or cloud their vision,
Or dull their hearing.

I have a Father
To whose councils you must submit.
I refer you to him
And his power to outwit
Every scheme of yours.
Not evident in the now
But ultimately somehow
They will be his.

Satan, you know where to go.
Just leave my kids behind.
The answer is still no.

CHAPTER NINE
He Is Very Jealous

In the final book of his space trilogy, *That Hideous Strength*, C. S. Lewis tells the story of a prickly young woman named Jane. She and her husband are both academians caught up in an Armageddon-like battle between good and evil on the campus of a British university. In the rarified, academic atmosphere of Jane's world, there is no tolerance for God or obedience to any authority. Although the book was written in the late 1940s, it uncannily describes the mind-set of many students and faculty on college campuses today. A complicated series of events lead to Jane's inclusion in the household of a Mr. Fisher-King. Toward the end of the book, Mr. Fisher-King, "the Director," asks Jane to pledge obedience to God. She has made peace with the need for obedience in her world, but God is another matter. She proclaims that she knows nothing of God but will pledge obedience to Mr. Fisher-King. His answer walks a delicate tightrope:

> *"It is enough for the present," said the Director. "This is the courtesy of Deep Heaven: that when you mean well, He always takes you to have meant better than you know. It will not be enough for always. He is very jealous. He will have you for no one but Himself in the end. But for tonight, it is enough."*[3]

Because it is easy to be lulled into complacency by the grace period of "for tonight, it is enough," and because we love our children, it is possible to trivialize the sin in their lives. We don't want to see it for what it is or what it has wrought in their relationship with God. In Ezekiel 8, God gives the prophet a vivid vision of the idolatry and perversion taking place among his people and in his

47

temple. In Ezekiel 8:17 he asks, "Have you seen this, son of man? Is it a trivial matter for the house of Judah to do the detestable things they are doing here?" (NIV).

Denial is a dangerous draught parents can all too easily drink. We would much rather call the old-fashioned sin in our children's lives something less bitter. We would love to pretend it—whatever "it" is—is a trivial matter. What alternative do we have to the trivialization of sin? It is something much less comfortable. It is a jealous grief. In Ezekiel 9:3–4 God instructs an angel ("the man clothed in linen") to "go throughout the city of Jerusalem and put a mark on the foreheads of those who grieve and lament over all the detestable things that are done in it." This is not a mark of scorn, superiority, or judgment, but rather one of pain. As parents who grieve in this way, there are times when we have felt the burning presence of such a mark. Although our God is compassionate, merciful, and courteous, the sin in our lives and our children's lives is not trivial. It gives him good reason to be jealous.

The Fight

Because God will have our sons and daughters for no one but himself in the end, we must pray with all the colossal will to fight off a mother grizzly. But not only does our Lord want them for himself; another fiercely vies for their souls as well. First Peter 5:8–9 warns us to "Be sober! Be on the alert! Your adversary the Devil is prowling around like a roaring lion, looking for anyone he can devour. Resist him, firm in the faith" (HCSB). A self-protection mechanism in each of us drives us to fend off our enemies, but the parental propulsion to attack any enemy who would dare to devour our young is even stronger. The only time I have ever been consciously rude to one of our son's friends was when a known drug dealer in our suburban neighborhood had the gall to show up at our doorstep. The Mama Bear in me couldn't help but bare her teeth.

We all know mothers who have heightened senses of fight within them. The older kids on our street dubbed one of our neighbors "Officer Jones." She petitioned for speed bumps, called teenagers' parents if she spotted them driving too fast, and stood at the end of her driveway chastising drivers with a furious slow-down motion as they sped past. Even I was a little afraid of her, but I understood her vigilante spirit. Her home was located on a down-hill, blind bend in the road, and her small children played every day near that potentially dangerous road. In her fierce desire to protect her kids from danger, she deputized herself as the neighborhood traffic cop. Her purpose wasn't to make friends; it was to protect her children.

Many of the institutions of social change in our country were founded by mothers and fathers whose children were the victim of the evil their organizations fight. Mothers Against Drunk Driving, to name one, is the product of the fight that rose within the breast of an angry mother whose daughter was killed by a drunk driver. The television show *America's Most Wanted* was the brainchild of a man whose son was abducted and violently murdered. In these cases the fight produced something positive.

Most of us have little opportunity to fight the enemy at the gates of our homes, at least not by founding institutions or literally sweeping the evil influences away from our doorsteps. But we are called to fight—and to fight with a vicious vengeance. Our ultimate enemy is Satan and our battlefields are the closets in which we pray. He wants our children for himself as surely as the most predatory human alive.

Tightly Shut Gates

Some days the seemingly gravitational pull Satan has on our children's lives can send us into despair. It seems that there is no Christian influence in their lives, while the forces in their environment—television, the Internet, movies, and friends—have an untold weight of influence. Our desolation renders us barely able to fight. One day my despair and God's Word had a head-on collision. It seemed to me that morning that Matt's life was shut tight and that God had lost the key to the entrance. In fact, from where I sat, it looked as if Satan had slipped in the back door and was taunting me through the window. He had gained access, and I had absolutely none. I opened my Bible to Joshua 6 thinking hopeless, angry thoughts. There I read, "The LORD said to Joshua, 'I have given you Jericho'" (v. 2 NLT). But the gates to the city were "tightly shut" (v. 1). This was the sort of oxymoron

I could relate to that day. A few days before I had been immensely encouraged by Jeremiah 30:10 (NASB):

Fear not, O Jacob, My servant, declares the LORD.
And do not be dismayed, O Israel;
For behold, I will save you from afar
And your offspring from the land of their captivity.
(author's emphasis)

Today my focus was more fixed on the land of my son's "captivity" than on the hope of a rescue. I don't remember why I had strayed so far in my thinking from the promise in Jeremiah 30, but I had, and it was difficult to see anything but the "tightly shut" gates of Matt's life. I read about the daily march of God's people around Jericho. I wondered if they ever passed by those gates and doubted that they would ever enter them. If they had doubts, they didn't voice them. Verse 10 tells us they were instructed to observe absolute silence during the march. On the seventh day the army marched seven times around the still-shut city. I read Joshua 6:20 and found the encouragement I needed to fight that day:

So the people shouted, and priests blew the trumpets; and when
the people heard the sound of the trumpet, the people shouted
with a great shout and the wall fell down flat, so that the people
ran right into the city, every man straight ahead, and they took
the city. (NASB)

In the New Testament, Jesus promises us a spiritual victory in prayer that is as real a conquest as the military charge against Jericho. Matthew 16:18–19 says, "On this rock I will build My church, and the forces of Hades will not overpower it. I will give you the keys of the kingdom of heaven, and whatever you bind on earth will have been bound in heaven, and whatever you loose on earth will have been loosed in heaven" (HCSB).

Like Jericho, the fortresses of Satan that threaten to imprison our sons and daughters may look tightly shut, but they are not. Satan and any of the tools he uses against our sons and our daughters can infuriate us. And that fury has a place to go: prayer. The prayers for my children, more than any other of my prayers, most resemble the marching and shouting of the Israelites at Jericho. When the deliverance of our children is at stake, prayer can take on the determination of a march and the passion of a shout.

The Courtesy of Deep Heaven

We cannot love both God and our children without the keen awareness of his jealousy—for their hearts and for ours. But neither can we love him and them without experiencing the tug-of-war that exists between his courtesy and his jealousy. When I pray for our sons, I beg God for his mercy, his courtesy. I used to say to him, "Come, Lord Jesus." Now I say, "Wait, please, Lord. Some of my loved ones are not yet safe."

A reading of the siege of Jericho is not complete without a consideration of its most famous citizen, Rahab. Like C. S. Lewis's Jane, she meant well and was able to place her trust in the messengers of a God she did not yet know. But at first glance, what I see within those doomed, tightly shut walls is a woman who was certainly not an Israelite—not by birth, not by morality, and not by indoctrination. She seems to belong in the ill-fated city of Jericho rather than among the holy army of Israel. Her destiny—to die beneath the rubble of Jericho's ruins—seems sure. With a little imagination I can see my own rebellious child in Rahab:

- Imprisoned, as it were, within the enemy's camp
- Morally and spiritually compromised by constant exposure to that enemy
- Singled out for a daring delivery by a God who is both courteous and jealous
- Surrounded by a marching, shouting army of praying believers

Perhaps the most heartening and hallowed task the Israelites performed on that seventh day of marching was the rescue of Rahab and her family. As I march out in prayer against an enemy whose walls cannot help but fall before my shouts of prayer, I can be comforted in the fact that my Commanding Officer is the same one whose battle plan included Rahab. He is compassionate and will not annihilate the enemy before rescuing those I love from that enemy's clutches.

QUESTIONS FOR REFLECTION

1. Recall a time when someone you love was hurt, criticized, or threatened. Do you remember experiencing the Mama Bear syndrome?
2. Describe the colossal will to fight for him or her that rose up within you.
3. How can that fury to fight be directed into your prayer life?
4. How does it encourage you to pray when you consider that God promises us victory over "the gates of hell" (Matt. 16:18 KJV)?

CHAPTER TEN
How Long a Wait?

W e are sitting in the dark. I gradually become aware of the person chewing gum behind me and the insufferable lack of legroom in front. When did the air-conditioning vent begin to blow a frigid blast on the back of my neck? I am beginning to feel an awkwardness, a vague embarrassment for the inept stagehands that have kept us waiting. Surely the curtain should have risen fifteen minutes ago. An entire mass of concertgoers squirm collectively as minutes tick by. We attempt to synchronize our watches with our tickets, and the exercise only increases our chagrin. No explanation, no apology is offered. The murmuring is fast becoming a low roar when, at last, we hear the musicians settle into their places, the pulleys grind, and a dim light grows more and more focused on the space beneath the gathers of the rising curtain. Finally, the wait is over.

Most of our waiting is just about as innocuous as that. When will the entertainment begin? When will our waitress bring the food? When will the light change? When will the package arrive? When will the next good thing happen? Something in us counts the cars on the train in anticipation of driving over the tracks. The longer the train, the more we feel victimized by the wait. In cities, short bouts of intense waiting often bring out the worst in us. We are never static, always dynamic, and the imposition of a delay rattles us. But delays are inevitable: the prescription isn't ready, the traffic thwarts us, the product is back-ordered, and the drive-through line is seven cars long. Staying peaceful and gracious as we hurtle through our days at breakneck speed requires an urban godliness which, when achieved, can send out the aroma of Christ to an impatient world.

But parenting is a different kind of waiting altogether. We begin waiting for a first smile, first tooth, first word, and end waiting for character to develop, right choices to be made, habits that seem to have atrophied to reemerge. Parenting teenagers who wander is such an excruciating form of waiting that it really should be assigned another word. If we counted the train cars along this road, we would never survive. We may not be able to count each car, but the rumble of the passing locomotive rings in our ears and shakes us to the core. Perhaps because we live in a world where waiting has been redefined by the microwave and high-speed Internet, the long, slow, "hang in there" aspect of parenting has become harder.

Three Days' Journey

Someone once told me that my son needed to be my "Isaac," offered to God on my own personal altar. I absorbed that truth about as glibly as "God is love." Who was she to tell me to offer my son to the Lord when I had done that every day of his life? Then I reread Genesis 22 and noticed something that shook my impatient heart. Abraham determined to obey God, to offer his son, his very life, on the appointed mountain. And it took him *three whole days* to get there! Three days to keep his deadly purposes to himself. Three days to imagine the deed. Three days to question God. Three days to hurt and agonize. Three days to say a silent good-bye to his innocent son. All on a desolate mountain road without the comfort of his family surrounding him.

When our "Isaac" was in eighth grade, my husband came to me with an encouraging word from the Lord. During his prayer time that morning, he sensed the Lord reassuring him that he would ultimately prevail in our son's life. I hugged that thought to myself the moment he shared it with me. "But," my husband said, "I believe things will get worse before they get better." At that time *worse* was difficult for me to imagine, so I soaked up that part of the message like a dry sponge. The next day the middle school principal called. Our son and two friends were caught dialing 911 from the school pay phone. The three-days' suspension that followed was clearly, to me, the "worse" God warned us about. I naively filed the experience away and said, "Whew, that's over. Now I'm ready for you to do your thing, Lord!" I probably don't need to tell you that my neat timetable became a mess over the next few months . . . and then years. Waiting for God to intervene meant staying up at night waiting for a runaway to come home (he didn't until the next afternoon), waiting for a drug test which he failed, waiting for a phone call, for a diagnosis, and then more waiting.

During the final trimester of pregnancy, I always enjoyed quoting, "O God, hasten to deliver me" (Ps. 70:1 NASB). Thankfully, the agenda of pregnancy and delivery is dictated by a defined gestation period. When I am impatient for the baby to arrive, to see my feet again, for my rings to fit my fingers again, my impatience has a narrow margin of time in which to wait. Not so with our teenagers or adult children. The Alpha and Omega, the Beginning and the End, knows how long we will have to wait. But we are usually not privy to that information. Our personal three-days' journey may be three months, three years, or even thirty. We may live life at the whirling pace of most, but stop us and ask the real questions about our "Isaac," and time stands still. We are waiting. Nothing in today's world has prepared us to wait in this way. But if God has required it, then, like Abraham, somehow we can do it.

What Is the Name of Your Altar?

Abraham left Mount Moriah minus the kindling for his sacrifice but with Isaac intact. As he left, he assigned a name to the altar site: "Jehovah Jireh, the Lord will provide" (Gen. 22:14 NIV). On the surface the meaning of this name is clear. Jehovah provided the sacrifice, the ram. This provision reverberates forward through Scripture and tells us God will provide Christ as our living sacrifice. But I can imagine that every fiber of Abraham's father heart felt the Lord's provision. The wherewithal to make the dreaded three-day trip, the courage to obey a God whose command he didn't understand, the words to answer his bewildered son—all were provided by Jehovah Jireh.

This naming of altars is fairly commonplace in the Old Testament. "Altars were places where the divine and human worlds interacted. Altars were places of exchange, communication, and influence. God responded actively to altar activity."[4] Twice Hagar fled Sarah's mistreatment only to end at an altar in the desert. She called the well where God met her Beer Lahai Roi, which means,

"The God who sees" (Gen. 16:14 NIV). After defeating the Amalekites, "Moses built an altar and called it The LORD is my Banner" (Exod. 17:15 NIV). Jehovah Nissi is at once God's name and a statement that "The LORD is my Banner." Fearful, tentative Gideon had an encounter in which God spoke peace to him. He called the altar he built Jehovah Shalom, "The LORD is Peace" (Judg. 6:24 NIV). That peace enabled Gideon to proceed with some rather daring exploits. Today we might say he "stepped outside of his comfort zone."

Notice that the names assigned to these holy places of inter-action between God and his people are synonyms for God himself. One would think Hagar might name the well, "My sorrow is all Sarah's fault!" Moses' altar was built where he stood for hours on end watching the battle with his arms raised high. He might have named the spot, "My arms ache." There are places on my map as a parent where I have met with God for the express purpose of venting my pain and anger. Some of those places have become holy altars where he spoke and I left with his name and character etched in my heart. Like Gideon, I have approached him with abject terror and left knowing his peace.

One such encounter took place on Stone Mountain near our home. We had just enrolled Matt in a drug rehab program. For the next few months he would still be at home, but the program would impose an almost cultlike control over him—over his time, his friendships, his interests. As he put it, to get sober he had to pitch all his old baggage out of the backseat of his car. At that time I mistrusted *everyone* in his most recent past, so I was more than willing to assist with any baggage pitching. On the Saturday before the program was to begin, my husband and I drove Matt and his best friend to the mountain so they could say a farewell of sorts. It turns out that this friend was not a drug user, but we did not know that at the time. Matt and his friend started up the walking path, and Bill and I followed. It didn't take long for them to put considerable distance between us. Every time Matt disappeared over a rise or around a bend, I panicked. I imagined an exchange of money and drugs. The experience of following our son up that mountain stressed just how frightened and frantic I had become. Was I going to be on a stakeout outside his room every night for the next five years? Was I going to bug his phone, read his mail, dog his every step? I realized I could not. At that moment I encountered "the God who sees." Contrary to what every cookie-jar-raiding toddler believes, moms do *not* have eyes in the backs of their heads. I was no exception. But God *sees*. Not only does he see, but he also provides what I need to trust his vision, including the internal peace to rest in him. All these things are true about God for me and for my children. The walk back down the mountain was full of peace. Nothing about our circumstances had changed. Meeting God there changed me.

Altars are the places where God gives us the perspective we need. Most days life looks like a reflection in one of those distorted state fair mirrors. Sometimes our bent-out-of-shape perspective is humorous, but usually it is just bent out of shape and needs to be ironed back into shape. In Psalm 73, the psalmist ponders the life of ease the ungodly seem to enjoy. The world looks out of focus to him. "When I tried to understand all this, it was oppressive to me till I entered the sanctuary of God; then I understood" (vv. 16–17 NIV). I am convinced that my perspective regarding my children remains skewed until I enter the sanctuary of his presence, offer them to him on his altar, and affirm his name and his character. It is only then that I can walk away saying, "Then I understood."

QUESTIONS FOR REFLECTION

1. When have you offered your son or daughter to God? Are there places and times you can remember?
2. How has God met you at your altar?
3. What have you learned as you have waited on the Lord there?
4. What aspect of his character has been affirmed to you?

CHAPTER ELEVEN
A Prayer Adventure

W e needed a new car. *New* has always meant "used but new to us" in the Murray vocabulary. My husband was about to graduate from seminary, and we had a brand-new baby who needed to be ferried about in a newer, larger, safer vehicle. A friend loaned Bill an ancient VW bug for a few months so that Matt and I didn't have to stay cooped up in our apartment every day. The bug honked every time it turned right, and since Bill drove it in a sharp right turn every day past a putting green, the car literally had enemies. One day after a long day at school, Bill approached it in the parking lot only to discover that the battery had fallen through the rusty undercarriage onto the pavement. We needed a car!

So we began to pray. In this particular instance we decided to pray specifically; in fact we sensed God prompting us to do so. We had two thousand dollars in the bank—inheritance money—but that wasn't enough. So we prayed first for enough money. Then we decided to pray for a station wagon. That wagon soon became, on our prayer list, a 1978 Ford Fairmont wagon, yellow, with wood-grain paneling (we didn't like any of the other colors). We prayed from September until the week of graduation in December.

On Monday of graduation week, we still had just two thousand dollars and no car. We were beginning to wonder if our praying had been amiss. That afternoon we got a phone call from our Southern Baptist seminary in Texas, telling us there was a five hundred dollar check waiting for us from a Catholic organization in Georgia. (We still can't figure that one out.) On Tuesday we received one hundred dollars tucked inside a note allegedly written by Bill's parents' dog. On Wednesday we received a check for two hundred twenty-five dollars from an equally obscure, unexpected source. Wednesday

58

night we bought a paper and scanned the classifieds. "1978 Ford Fairmont wagon—$2,850" jumped off the newsprint at us. If you did the math, you know that's exactly what we had. No less, no more. On Thursday we bought our car, which, by the way, was yellow with wood-grain paneling. On Friday Bill graduated, and the three of us promptly put eight hundred plus miles on our "new" car.

One epilogue to this story is that we spent the week after Christmas interviewing with a church we had assumed would be our next move. Several days into the interview process, we became certain this was not the place for us. So we drove back to Texas from the East Coast with our new baby, facing the new year with no job and no prospects. But the wheels that ferried us reminded us mile after mile that God, while unpredictable, is always faithful.

That's Not All of the Story

I hesitate to recount such a dramatic answer-to-prayer story because I'm afraid it could be a misrepresentation. First, it misrepresents me. For every time I have had a prayer encounter like that one, I have either neglected to pray and fretted instead; or I have prayed outlandishly wrong; or I have prayed but flagged in my efforts so that, by the time the prayer was answered, I missed it. Our car story is more consistent with God's character than it is with mine.

I'm also afraid prayer itself may be misrepresented by that story. In some ways I'm tempted to believe that the dramatic, specific nature of our experience was calculated by a wise Father who knew what utter babies we were. Our nascent faith needed the boost. Over the years I've come to experience prayer more as a conversation than a negotiation, and I'm convinced the initiator of that conversation is always God, not me. His Word, seen this way, is the start of a conversation, a tête-à-tête in which he pours out his desires, his love, his plans, and we respond in kind. One of his beginning lines is, "Cast your cares on [me]" (1 Peter 5:7 HCSB). In these words I learn that I can tell him my needs and the needs of those I love. I am merely responding to his request in doing so. On any given day, he may say to me words like, "Be kind and compassionate to one another, forgiving one another" (Eph. 4:32 HCSB), and that is my cue to confess an unkind word or an unforgiving spirit. Or I may hear him say, "Don't worry about anything; instead pray about everything. Tell [me] your needs and don't forget to thank [me] for [my] answers" (Phil. 4:6 TLB). The appropriate response to him is to pour out my "everything." Prayer that is just a list to be checked off reduces intimate fellowship with God to a formula in which we mechanically plug in certain factors and God cranks out the answers.

God's character could be misconstrued if viewed solely through the lens of answered prayer. Let it never be said that Bill and I controlled God's actions by our specific prayers for a new car. To prove that we cannot dictate God's plans, it might help to see a few other answers to prayers from my past. In college I explained to God in great detail why I would not marry until I was thirty-five years old. And I would appreciate it if you would work that out, God, thank you very much. When I was twenty-one, I met Bill and fell so hard I still can't see straight. I assumed we would have girls, so that's how I prayed. I envisioned tea parties and crafts and dress-up. One by one these rip-roarin' boys entered our lives, and I have discovered that soccer in the front yard is a lot more satisfying than tea parties in the living room could ever be! The bottom line is that God is in control and I am not. Prayer must always take that into account.

Finally, life itself can be misrepresented by a tidy story of answered prayer. Sometimes we pray for the best and get what seems to be the worst. William Penn said, "May we not despise or oppose what we do not understand." Easier said than done. There are all too many opportunities in life, especially the life of a parent, to despise or oppose the things we can't control.

Fear of the Worst

I spoke at a women's luncheon about prayer and, specifically, prayer for our families. Most of the women there were grandmothers, so I knew I could not candy-coat prayer for them, but I wanted to encourage them. I told them about our yellow station wagon, and I also told them some of our struggles. One sweet, older lady sat down next to me as the others were leaving. She said, "You know, my son and daughter-in-law went through a long, difficult time with their son."

I began to ask a polite question, but she went on, "He took his life."

There, she said it. And I've typed it. The thing I fear most, the thing I beg God to spare us from. The thought can send my pulse racing and stop my heart all at once.

I don't think I'm the only parent who has moments of irrational fear. For me, this usually occurs at night. Late one night I had a conversation on the phone with one of our sons in which I just listened for a long time as he expressed his discouragement about a problem. His words said little, but the tone of his voice spoke volumes. My husband says I am addicted to closure. If that's true (it is), a distance of several hundred miles between a struggling child and me can send me up the wall. I wanted to pray with our son, to give him miraculously wise counsel. I wanted to hear the weight lifted from his voice. But I didn't. We hung up, and I went into a tailspin. Everything in me wanted to call him back or to coerce Bill into checking on him later that night. I even considered driving the four hours to see him. I began imagining his despair taking on such gigantic proportions that he would choose the path that kindly grandmother's grandson took.

I went through the routines of bedtime with an inner panic that kept me from doing what I really needed to do. Finally I got to my knees. In an instant I knew God was speaking to me about, not my son, but me. My fears needed tending to more than his dilemma did. He spoke; I listened. Then, without the panic, I told him my concerns for our son. I didn't make that check-up call. I was reminded of the mother who was weary with worry and waiting up for a child to come home. As she waited, she heard the Lord say, "You go on to bed. I'll wait up." I think the Lord "checked up" that night for me. Our son called a few days later, and the problem was already a faint memory.

Epilogue, Number Two

That yellow station wagon was with us for a long time. Four years later Matt, a precocious four-year-old by then, somehow got it into gear and coasted it down our steep driveway, slamming it into the neighbor's house. Both Matt and the car survived without a scratch, but I can't say the same for our neighbor's house! We kept the car for several years after that. The next station wagon lasted even longer. In the meantime I still pray for specifics. Most of our vehicles have been answers to prayers. Now that teenagers drive them, I pray in other ways about cars. And I still ask God to spare us from "the worst," whatever that happens to look like at the time. But praying for our children day in and day out, throughout the moments of their lives, is nothing like praying for a new car. One look at the pain in a grandmother's eyes is enough to remind me. Prayer is a holy calling, a deep dialogue, a relationship, a bond between those who pray and the King of heaven who starts the conversation to begin with.

QUESTIONS FOR REFLECTION

1. Recollect a specific answer to prayer from your past. How did it encourage your faith at the time?
2. How can you begin to view Scripture as the beginning of a conversation between you and God?
3. What "conversation starters" has God begun with you lately?
4. What answers can you make to him?

CHAPTER TWELVE
A Defining Moment

There are sweet defining moments, and there are sour ones. This one started off sweet and ended on a sour note. Most of my defining moments are outwardly inconsequential, and this was no different. My oldest two children were a toddler and an infant, and we were strolling through the mall. I wasn't in a hurry or stressed, and they, as children will, reflected my calm. It was one of those simple-pleasure days. Nothing significant was happening, but I still remember the delight I felt in their sweet, cherubic faces and the fun we three had doing next to nothing.

We stopped to enjoy a frozen yogurt before heading home. I had noticed a kindly older gentleman watching us with a wistful look on his face. We settled with our yogurt next to the fountain where my oldest took great delight in tossing pennies and making childlike wishes. Soon the elderly man came to join us.

"Your boys are just beautiful," he commented.

"Thank you," I answered, beaming because I think they are too.

"They'll break your heart when they're older," he said. And the wistful look turned dark. I couldn't tell if his face registered bitterness or simply heartbreak, but I knew there was a deep, long story beneath his brief comment.

Just then the boys began to squirm, and I knew I had to leave. I found I was squirming too. The last thing I wanted to hear was how this sad old man's children, who had once been as innocent as mine, broke his heart. The possibility of such a thing burst the bubble of my day. Of my hopes and dreams. I murmured a quick, stranger's good-bye and left. We sang songs on the way home, and I forgot him.

But it is eighteen years later, and I have not forgotten. Why? Because I now know that a portion of a parent's love is pain. Not because sweet children go sour. They don't exactly—not in their parent's eyes. But they do have two things I refused to reckon with when they were young: a sin nature and a free will. One absolute my parents gave me and my children inherited from my husband and me. And one precious gift God bestowed upon all humanity, thus empowering his cherubic children to hurt him. C. S. Lewis understood the risks involved in love and the doom inherent when we avoid those risks:

> To love at all is to be vulnerable. Love anything, and your heart will certainly be wrung and possibly broken. If you want to make sure of keeping it intact, you must give your heart to no one, not even to an animal. Wrap it carefully round with hobbies and little luxuries; avoid all entanglements; lock it up safe in the casket or coffin of your selfishness. But in that casket—safe, dark, and motionless, airless—it will change. It will not be broken; it will become unbreakable, impenetrable, irredeemable. . . . The only place outside of Heaven where you can be perfectly safe from all the dangers of love is hell.[5]

Perhaps when 1 John 4:18 tells us that "there is no fear in love" (HCSB), this is, in part, the type of fear to which John refers.

Let's Be Honest

That word *honest* is perhaps the most frightening of words. If I am honest, I may be pressed to tell you how I really feel, how savagely angry I am, how much I can dislike my own child at times, how disloyal I feel toward my own kid or toward God himself. These feral emotions are the bones of the skeleton in my closet. I often feel ashamed of them and entitled to them all at once. My children *have* broken my heart. Unless they remain helpless infants, they are bound to do so to some degree. Sometimes the heartbreak is small, more a function of my own unrealistic expectations of them, but sometimes the hurt is understandable. When I talk to a parent whose child has seen the inside of a jail cell, whose son's girlfriend chose an abortion, whose daughter's drug habit is marking her beautiful eyes with dark circles, whose son's thieving is common knowledge in the neighborhood, whose daughter cannot see that she is literally wasting away in a sad attempt to be thin, this is what I hear:

"How did this happen?"

"Why is she wasting her life?"

"This is not what I thought parenting would be like!"

"What did we do wrong?"

"Why would he deliberately hurt us this way?"

"What have we done to deserve this?"

The words don't come anywhere near communicating the pain beneath them. The despair is locked away in an emotional dungeon where it remains docile most of the time; we couldn't function otherwise. But, until the child is safely home, the captive feelings can stir and whimper, begging to be released.

I am tempted to clean up the previous paragraph. Or to end with wise words that will cause hurting parents everywhere to vanquish the monster feelings that rumble and roar dangerously in their hearts' dungeons. There is the tendency to believe that hope cannot coexist with hurt, that faith means feeling faithful all the time. As believing parents, we can be duped into a sundial faith, one that only values or measures the sunny hours. In my most noble moments, those when the dungeon is locked up tight, its walls fortified so that I can't hear the hurt in the cellar of my heart, I can cry out to God as did the saints of old:

Teach us, Lord,
to serve you as you deserve,
to give and not to count the cost,
to fight and not to heed the wounds,
to toil and not to seek for rest,
to labour and not to ask for any reward
save that of knowing that we do your will.
—Ignatius Loyola (1491–1556)

Can such sentiments coexist alongside the raw emotions my heart regularly visits? Can I affirm my belief in a God who deserves to be served, given to and fought for, all the while taking such dramatic emotional detours? Are these emotions tantamount to disloyalty? Or, even worse, am I a hypocrite for feeling them?

Identification

Could it be that our pain over a struggling child is actually an honor, in that we are identifying with our Lord and his pain? I recall the conversation with a friend in college when I first grasped the concept of identification. I called my friend Roger late one night after a lively debate had occurred in my dorm room. Six or seven friends and I discussed God, truth, and morality into the wee hours of the night. Of all the opinions aired that night, mine were by far the most incendiary. Espousing a belief in a nameable God who required acknowledgment from his creation made me a laughing-stock and my words fighting words. Friends whose esteem I thought I had earned now eschewed not only my words but also me. I was a laughingstock, and it didn't feel very good; in fact, I was devastated. I called Roger hoping for a large dose of commiseration. I'll never forget his words, delivered over the phone in an almost celebratory tone, "Kitti, how exciting! You got to identify with the rejection of Christ tonight. What an honor!" Once I understood that the hurt I felt over being rejected by my friends was actually akin to Christ's pain, I was able to free those feelings from the dungeon to where they belonged: the throne room.

If a few college friends could wound me, then it is no wonder my heart aches over my children when they go astray. Listen to the Father in Hosea 11:8. He sounds an awful lot like us: "How can I give you up, Ephraim? How can I hand you over? . . . My heart is changed within me; and my compassion is aroused" (NIV). The cry of God's heart in this instance is born of a parental disappointment in his errant child. "When Israel was a child, I loved him, and out of Egypt I called my son. But the more I called Israel, the further they went from me. . . . It was I who taught Ephraim to walk, taking them by the arms; but they did not realize it was I who healed them" (Hos. 11:1–3 NIV). Here we see a Father God who has great love and high hopes for his son, only to watch that son dash his hopes. I can relate. And that is a privilege.

Co-Passion

If we are honored in those rare moments when we identify with God's heart, *his* desire to identify with *us* is an even greater blessing.

In Isaiah 54, God likens his people to (take your pick) a widow, a wife unable to bear children, or an abandoned wife. He offers soothing words to this sad group of lonely-hearts club members. "For a brief moment I abandoned you, but with deep compassion I will bring you back. In a surge of anger I hid my face from you for a moment, but with everlasting kindness I will have compassion on you" (vv. 7–8 NIV). Like Hosea, Isaiah writes a message from a compassionate God.

Have you ever heard someone say to you, "I know how you feel," and, because they did *not* know how you felt, the words sounded like fingernails on a chalkboard? While the platitude can ring false, the tonic our feelings so desperately need is genuine identification. In rare moments a friend may know exactly how you feel; that is comforting. In even more rare moments, someone may feel *with* you; that is compassion. *Co* means "with" and *passion* means "feeling." This is what God willingly promises to do for us, to feel *with* us. While we may have experiences here and there of identification with him, he is always about the mission of feeling with us. His love for us carries with it a heavenly wideness that absorbs our pain and pleasure in its wake.

God's compassion for me gives me the courage to unlock the monster in the dungeon. Hurt, anger, and disappointment are so thick in the atmosphere of my heart at times that I am afraid I will never see clearly again if I let them escape. But to know I will never feel them alone siphons off a good deal of the dread. When my husband was thirty-eight, he suffered a massive heart attack and was airlifted to a hospital 120 miles away from our home, where he spent nine days in a cardiac critical care unit. The first night, as I waited for some word from the doctor, I was surrounded by friends who held my hand and prayed with me until they, one by one, left for the long trek back to their homes. I spent the first night in a CCU waiting room all alone. Someone had left me a Bible, so I kept my mind, heart, and eyes glued to its pages. I felt enveloped in a grace bubble where I could not have doubted God's presence if I had tried.

I spent the remainder of those nine nights in a hotel of sorts next door to the hospital. I'd like to say the grace bubble remained intact, but it didn't. Each morning I woke with feelings of panic that nearly paralyzed me. I would make a halfhearted attempt at breakfast before the sun came up, and then I would walk over to the hospital. I knew enough to know God's compassion was at my disposal, but I was afraid to go to him. I thought I might start blubbering and never stop. My husband needed me to be calm; my children, who were four, six, nine, and eleven, took their cues from me. I had to hold the family together. It wasn't until I finally found a place (hospitals don't have many tucked-away quiet spots) to succumb to my emotions before the Lord that I found relief. I discovered a bathroom in a wing of the hospital that was under construction. It was a private enough place for me to pour out my heart to God between the panic of breakfast and the vigil of the critical care unit. What did I say to God? I don't remember at all. I told him how I felt. What did God say to me? That I don't recall either, but I knew his compassion. He held me and felt my fear and pain. I cannot compose an outline of the biblical truths I learned, but those nine days marked a milestone of intimacy with my Savior in which he became dearer to me.

In one sense the pain we experience when our children hurt us embodies the gospel. We are broken and hurting, when along comes, not a knight on a fiery steed, but a Parent who is, like us, broken and hurting. His pain has a purpose: "The chastening for our well-being fell upon Him, and by His scourging we are healed" (Isa. 53:5 NASB). We may identify with him for a fleeting instant, but he doesn't just visit our sorrows, he carries them away. So that we might ultimately say a final farewell to suffering, "the LORD has caused the iniquity of us all to fall on Him" (Isa. 53:6 NASB). We may identify with him for a fleeting instant when our children cause us pain, but he doesn't stop at identification with our sorrows, he carries them away.

QUESTIONS FOR REFLECTION

1. Do you remember a time when your dreams for your child were dashed or dimmed?
2. Have you ever been ashamed of your feelings of disappointment regarding your children?
3. How can you be helped by the knowledge that you are identifying with a hurting God?
4. How can you enjoy his compassion in the midst of your pain?

Your Voice

O Lord,
I called my children
Home to you.
And I clanged;
Harsh, like the ring
Of a dinner bell
Across a still neighborhood.

O Lord,
I warned my children
Away from sin.
And I blared;
Sonorous, like the sound
Of a foghorn
On the wild open seas.

O Lord,
I woke my children
To your truth.
And I droned;
Persistent, like the buzz
Of an angry alarm clock
In the pale morning light.

O Lord,
The truth is worth knowing,
The danger worth averting
And the home
Worth the trip back.
Please tell them for me
In your own voice.

CHAPTER THIRTEEN
God, the Recycler

Have you ever noticed just how many words in Scripture begin with the prefix *re*? For example, to name only a few:

renew	redeem	reconcile
recover	reform	refine
refresh	repair	restore
return	revive	rebuild

Apparently God is in the business of redoing things. The unavoidable implication is that we, and our children, have the propensity to take something God has done and undo it. We take the creation he has made and unmake it. Silver becomes full of impurities and needs to be refined. New becomes old and must be renewed. A precious possession is sold and must be redeemed. A glorious temple is demolished and must be rebuilt. A valuable coin is lost and must be recovered. Fresh becomes stale and must be refreshed. You get the idea.

But do we? When it comes to our children, we tend to see a clean slate. It is because we knew them "back when" that we struggle when the slate becomes dirty, cracked, or even broken. We see back to the sweet innocence and, because we love them, we see forward to the fresh potential. We weren't born yesterday, so we know these sad truths as well: drugs can cause irrevocable damage, virginity cannot be regained, a police record doesn't just go away, and years lived in blatant sin cannot be relived. So, when we see our sons or daughters making these choices, we are apt to focus on the *un* and hardly believe in the hope of a *re*.

The Valley of Dry Bones

The capacity of a feature film to amaze us is increasing exponentially. Hollywood has capitalized on this fact by churning out remake after remake. The flight of a superhero over building tops looked suspect on the silver screen thirty years ago. Today we catch our breath as he soars through computer-generated airspace. Dinosaurs were more comical than creepy back then. Have you ever thought about some of the scenes in Scripture that would take a special effects team to reproduce? The crossing of the Red Sea, Elijah's flaming chariot, the singing of thousands of angels over a lonely hillside outside Bethlehem? These events are perhaps more imaginable today, thanks to the movie screen.

One Old Testament vision has all the makings of a horror film. In Ezekiel 37, the prophet Ezekiel is transported to a valley that is "full of bones" (v. 1 NASB). He reports that, "there were very many on the surface of the valley; and lo, they were very dry" (In other words, dead, dry, lo, very dry!). A recent film features the reconstruction and revitalization of mummies' bodies. The transformation is menacingly meticulous and takes most of the two hours to unfold. But in Ezekiel's vision the breath God sends resurrects the army of dry bones in an instant. Verse 10 tells us: "So I prophesied as He commanded me, and the breath came into them, and they came to life and stood on their feet, an exceedingly great army" (NASB). I can almost picture it as Ezekiel might have. Everywhere I step the dust of bones is one breath away from total oxidation. The atmosphere is tinged with the fine powder of human remains. And suddenly the air literally clears as men—whole, healthy, living men—arise!

A later prophet describes a reversal of this scene in a different place at a different time: "Their flesh will rot while they are still standing on their feet, their eyes will rot in their sockets, and their tongues will rot in their mouths" (Zech. 14:12 NIV). It is difficult not to view this as a scene right out of one of those eerie *Return of the Mummy* flicks. But this is the plight of enemies of the Lord during the last battles on earth. Ezekiel's vision was something altogether different, not a horde of staggering half-formed men but rather a living, breathing, resurrected army of hope.

In Ezekiel's day the people of God were moaning in despair: "Our bones are dried up and our hope has perished. We are completely cut off" (Ezek. 37:11 NASB). They were living life fully in the *un* of their own making. This is where my heart grasps Ezekiel's vision for itself. As parents, my husband and I have certainly felt that "our hope has perished." Sometimes this loss of hope is because I see the situation my child is in or the condition of his heart as a veritable pit of dry bones. My mind dwells with morbid tenacity on the mess his life is in. In doing so I cannot even imagine the miracles God can perform in fixing that mess. The phrase "dry bones" seems to exactly fit where we are. It speaks of a death beyond any hope of resuscitation.

"Now Everything Is Spoiled"

A friend of ours confided in us after discovering that her son had become sexually active. Her first reaction was to say, "Now everything is spoiled. He has lost his virginity and can't get it back." We couldn't help but agree. There will surely be consequences this boy will suffer either now or later or both. She is right to grieve. But this valley, though something in it has been murdered and is decaying, can come back to life. Listen to what God instructs Ezekiel to tell his people:

> "Behold, I will open your graves and cause you to come up out of your graves, My people; and I will bring you into the land of Israel. Then you will know that I am the LORD, when I have opened your graves and caused you to come up out of your graves, My people. I will put My Spirit within you and you will come to life. . . . Then you will know that I, the LORD, have spoken and done it," declares the Lord.
>
> (Ezek. 37:12–14 NASB)

The valley of dry bones can stir up my imagination when I struggle to believe God. Like my friend, I sometimes look at a choice one of my children has made and sigh, "Now everything is spoiled!" As a mother who has had the privilege to gaze on my children's faces when they were fresh and young and full of potential, I grieve when a wrong decision or lifestyle choice strips those faces of their innocence. In his classic poem *The Hound of Heaven*, Francis Thompson captures the conversation between a rebellious wanderer and a waiting God who robs us only for the purpose of blessing us in the end. In the beginning of the poem, the spiritual outlaw admits to a life bent unswervingly toward rebellion:

> I fled Him, down the nights and down the days;
>   I fled Him, down the arches of the years;
> I fled Him, down the labyrinthine ways
>   Of my own mind; and in the mist of tears
> I hid from Him, and under running laughter.
>   Up vistaed hopes, I sped;
>   And shot, precipitated,
> Adown Titanic glooms of chasmed fears,
>   From those strong Feet that followed after,
>   Followed after.

Before long, the wanderer cannot help but see the destruction this path has wrought upon his life. His self-portrait looks uncannily like the valley of dry bones:

> I stand amid the dust o' the mounded years—
> My mangled youth lies dead beneath the heap.
> My days have crackled and gone up in smoke,
> Have puffed and burst as sun-starts on a stream.

It is to this dry, barren heart that God speaks these words of redemption and love:

> All which I took from thee I did but take,
>   Not for thy harms,
> But just that thou might'st seek it in My arms.
>   All which thy child's mistake
> Fancies as lost, I have stored for thee at home:
>   Rise, clasp My hand, and come.[6]

The valley of dry bones reminds me that I too would be a mere breath of skeletal remains without his resurrecting breath. Here I see the truth that the things we unmake our Lord can remake. He delights in restoration. He relishes the thought of giving back what has been lost. In this valley God transforms my remorse into reconciliation, and rebellion is met with restoration. In it I see a largerthan-life screening of my dream. My wandering child, whose life carries with it the scent of death, is raised up by the breath of God! I can touch it, feel it, and smell it in the air.

QUESTIONS FOR REFLECTION

1. What are some things in your life or the life of your son or daughter that need to be remade by our Redeemer?
2. How has your hope been reduced to a valley of dry bones?
3. How can the biblical picture of bones coming back to life encourage your faith?
4. As in the valley of dry bones, how can God restore those mistakes and failures?

CHAPTER FOURTEEN
The Valley of Achor

While we're visiting valleys, let's stop by another. I encountered the Valley of Achor in the book of Hosea several years ago. In chapter 2 of that wonderful story of redemption, God woos his whoring bride. His love pours out of the verses as he sings a love song to her: "I will betroth you to me forever; I will betroth you in righteousness and justice, in love and compassion" (v. 19 NIV). He promises to "allure her" (v. 14 NIV) and to "speak kindly to her" (v. 14 NASB). In verse 15 he tells her he will turn her "Valley of Achor" into "a door of hope." *Achor* means trouble. If you have a son or daughter who is rebelling against you, God, or both, you have trouble. You are not necessarily *in* trouble, but you most certainly *have* trouble. You know what I mean. You may be literally paying for his mistakes through insurance, counseling, court fees, or medical bills. Your family life has been disrupted. You are thrust into crisis mode more often than is normal. The interaction in your home is strained, maybe even hostile. Life is no picnic. It is downright trouble! You love your son or your daughter so much that you would endure ten times as much trouble for his or her sake if you had to, but that doesn't make it any less what it is: trouble.

During troublesome times, I find it impossible not to connect our trouble to my own failures and weaknesses. If only I had been more patient or more kind, if I had prayed more or been less strict. If only I had made wiser decisions. There must be heaping amounts of blame to be had, and I deserve my share! Many times when I have asked God to turn our family's valley of trouble into a door of hope, I have thought, *Why should God come to our rescue when we bring most of this trouble on ourselves?* Even so, I realize this promise is written by a loving Husband to a bride who commits adultery again and again. If a prostitute can walk through the door of hope, then surely it is not open only to the deserving.

Not long ago I decided to look more closely at the Valley of Achor since I seemed to spend so much time in it. I discovered that it refers to an actual valley. Hundreds of years before Hosea's day, after their parents wandered in the desert for forty years, the Israelites began their conquering march into Canaan. Early in the campaign they were defeated at a town called Ai because of the sin of a man named Achan. The account in Joshua 7 begins with this ominous introduction: "But the Israelites acted unfaithfully in regard to the devoted things" (v. 1 NIV). Every bit of the plunder was to be dedicated to the Lord, but Achan secretly kept some hidden away for himself. The valley in which Achan was stoned for his sin was called Achor. Here's what I learned in that disreputable valley about self-imposed trouble:

Sin Causes Trouble

In Joshua 7:25 (NASB) we find Joshua saying to Achan, "Why have you troubled us? The LORD will trouble you this day." These words preceded the stoning of Achan and his family. While I can't fully grasp the type of violent justice so prevalent in the Old Testament, it is clear to me that sin, hidden or open, causes trouble. Not only did Achan's actions result in his own punishment, but also the presence of sin in the camp hobbled the army of Israel so that what should have been a swift victory ended in defeat. The battle between Israel and Ai was like a matchup between the five-A state champs and a last-place single-A team, it should have been no contest.

One Christmas a friend of ours was surprised when the memory of the trouble her daughter had caused their family years before reared its ugly head. She found it didn't take much to open those old wounds. Her daughter flew into town for the holidays with several high-maintenance pets and a rather imperious expectation that everyone accommodate her entourage. Like the stabbing ghost pains an amputee feels from a limb that isn't there, the hassle those pets brought into their home, while benign, stirred up old, familiar feelings from earlier years. When their daughter was a young teenager, her rebellion cost the family many sleepless nights and plenty of turmoil. The trouble my friend experienced at the hands of her young daughter seems small compared to the savage penalty Achan and the Israelites endured, but the emotional toll was enough to reverberate in her family years afterward.

Sin Provokes God's Wrath

This story makes the fact of God's anger against sin inescapable; to use Joshua's term, it is "fierce" (Josh. 7:26 NIV). When one of our sons was somewhere between eighteen and twenty, an adult, I realized that I was praying only "mother" prayers for him. I wanted him to be protected, to feel good about himself, to succeed. At that point I consciously released him to be dealt with by God as his Father. I saw that, while God's love is as tender as a mother's, it is also "fierce" as a father's. Just as a young man who is a mama's boy is soft and ill prepared for the tough spots of life, so I knew it was time for my son to transition spiritually from mama's boy to the son of his Father. The same can be said for girls. A young woman who is coddled and never made to feel the consequences of her behavior will not be mature enough to walk into the adult roles in life. A wise father balances wrath and tenderness.

Escape from God's Wrath

Before leaving the valley, Joshua tells us, "They raised over him a great heap of stones that stands to this day, and the LORD turned from the fierceness of His anger" (v. 26 NASB). Here's where the story gets so much better. The truth is that we are all Achans, and we all deserve an eternity of God's wrath. Isaiah 53:6 tells us that "the Lord has caused [heaped] the iniquity of us all on Him." The heaping of punishment on Jesus at the cross was for the Achans of the world. That includes me, my family, all of humankind. We have sinned and in our sinning brought trouble upon ourselves. But now, in Christ, instead of saying, "The LORD will trouble you this day" (Josh. 7:25 NASB), God says, "I will heal their apostasy, I will love them freely, For My anger has turned away from them" (Hos. 14:4 NASB).

The Transformation of Trouble

During his ninth-grade year, our son David transferred to a different school so that he could play football. On his first day at the new school, he knew he had made a mistake. To his credit he stuck it out for six long months in a situation that was far less than best. Adjusting to new classes, losing eligibility for varsity sports when he went back to his old school the next year, and trying to make new friends and keep old friends, all stirred up trouble. Several months after that difficult experience, he began quoting Psalm 119:71: "It was good for me that I was afflicted, so that I may learn Your statutes" (NASB). His trouble—enduring it and dealing with it—became a doorway into turbo charged character growth and deeper intimacy with the Lord. The same was true for the Israelites at Achor. They were victorious in subsequent battles after the debacle at Ai. A dry, hopeless valley of trouble and defeat can truly become "a door of hope."

Valleys

When I mapped out my life, I never planned to visit valleys, much less spend time camping out in them. But when I am there, I find I am in good company. Ezekiel tells me the people of God found renewal in the valley of dry bones. Psalm 23 reminds me that David was familiar with the valley of the shadow of death and was not afraid of it. In Psalm 84, the Sons of Korah sang of passing "through the Valley of Baca" (v. 6 NIV). *Baca* means tears. Like other valley travelers before them, these psalmists observed that tours through this valley of tears are temporary. Tears in this valley eventually become early rain, a spring that "covers it with blessings" (Ps. 84:6 NASB). I am thankful for my excursions to the Valley of Achor. There I can see trouble dissolve into a doorway. I can walk through that door, knowing that God is about the business of redoing what has been done wrongly apart from him.

QUESTIONS FOR REFLECTION

1. What does the valley you've been in lately resemble?
2. What trouble has been introduced into your family life?
3. How can you find a door of hope in your valley?
4. How does this door of hope help you to pray for your son or daughter?

CHAPTER FIFTEEN
The Ultimate Taste Test

I could get on a 747, fly to France, buy the most delectable pastry there, fly back, deliver it hot and fresh to my kids, and they would invariably turn up their noses and ask for a Pop-Tart. If it has the words *whole grain, natural,* or *unsweetened* in it, they don't want it! And I have a hunch this preference for the prepackaged, artificially colored and flavored is a universal pattern in most children. I've yet to see children queue up to a salad bar when pizza or hamburgers are on the menu. The house that gives out apples or raisins at Halloween is usually first on the boycott list. And I've rarely seen a vegetable plate listed on a children's menu.

Universal or not, I still wish I did a better job of teaching my kids to eat right. Our oldest child didn't taste sugar until he was three. The fourth had cotton candy before he had teeth! When they were young, isolation worked. I just kept all that evil junk outside of their realm of experience. They never knew what they were missing. But friends, birthday parties, fast food between ball games, drivers' licenses and, ultimately, autonomy have thwarted all my efforts at fostering nutritional purity.

Since I couldn't keep them from the world of Twinkies and sodas, it just made sense to work hard at making "mom food" competitive. Doesn't it stand to reason that a home-cooked meal followed by home-baked dessert would easily trump chicken nuggets and a milkshake? No such luck. I can't spend the billions on advertising, and I'm not sure I want to stock my pantry with the dyes, oils, and chemicals I suspect the competition uses.

As a last-ditch effort, I thought education would work. But telling my teenager about the nutritional evils of processed food is like telling him not to wear a hat because it might make him bald

79

when he's fifty or warning him of *any* danger that has effects beyond right this minute. The "I'm going to live forever" syndrome seeps into the kitchen in the home where teenagers live. Besides, whether I am perpetuating a myth or propounding a fact, it seems my "wisdom" is all the same to them.

The bottom line is: junk food tastes good, and often wholesome food does not. I have a feeling, based on my own experience, that my boys will eventually alter their eating habits at least somewhat for the better. Expanding waistlines, aging bodies, and persistent wives will cause them to wise up. Wisdom will supercede taste to some degree. In fact, a burgeoning attention to nutrition has been introduced to their consciousness through the door of athletics.

But what about the spiritual diet? Will isolation from junk, education, and an attempt to make spiritual things "taste better" than the things of the world cause my sons to choose the right spiritual diet? When it comes to spiritual matters, what and how do I serve my kids?

If I Be Lifted Up

We live in a large southern city that is saturated with churches. Every nuance of every denomination exists here. Any size, any theological flavor, any possible worship style, and any type of preaching can be found within a reasonable driving distance from any home. Consequently we have become ecclesiastical gourmands, fastidiously tasting from a dozen kitchens before our discerning palates choose to settle at one dining table. Nowhere is this finicky church-chooser mentality more apparent than in parents of teenagers. A friend's family arrived from another city and asked about churches. The first, and often only, report she heard from person after person was, "We have a great youth group." Many times this comment would be followed by a litany of all the great activities with which said youth group filled their family calendar. My friend was dismayed that these reports lacked any reference to the church's teaching of the Word, to their love for one another, or to outreach into the community.

The prevailing sentiment *seems* to be that our kids will love Jesus if we cart them off to a great youth group or, better yet, ante up for a Christian school. The insidious lie in all this is that Jesus will not be appealing to my kids unless I present him to them through these mediums. The unbearable onus for us parents is that we will fail to lead our children to Christ if we don't orchestrate a convincing song and dance for them.

Moses employed a different strategy. Remember the snakes in the desert? Venomous serpents plagued the Israelites while they were wandering with Moses in the desert. It took quite a few deaths from snakebites before the leaders approached Moses for help. He fashioned a bronze serpent, held it up on a standard, and all who looked on it were healed. The lifting up of that serpent makes no sense to today's church consumer. Was no social program enacted for snakebite victims? Was there no soothing music to accompany the lifting of the bronze standard? What about a seminar on how to avoid snakebites altogether? What about small groups for survivors to process their experiences?

Of all the miracles recorded of those years, the snake on a stick seems to be one of the least auspicious, but a thousand years later Jesus referred to that simple antidote: "As Moses lifted up the serpent in the desert, so the Son of Man must be lifted up, so that everyone who believes in Him may have eternal life" (John 3:14–15 NIV). No song and dance here. The "lifting up" Jesus was probably referring to was the manner of his death. If so, the plain directive to us is to look upon him and believe in his impalement for our healing. Even the "lifting up" of our Savior has already been accomplished. Numbers 21 does not tell us whether *every* person dying with snake venom coursing through his veins took advantage of the healing offered by Moses. I wonder if there weren't some who were offended by the simplicity of healing at a glance. Some may have perished while pursuing a more complicated cure.

Might I have been one of those? It seems I take the crystal clear message of Jesus and complicate it at every turn. His "recipe," if you will, is unencumbered by confusing directions or exotic elements. It has one pure ingredient: himself. I am prone to add a dash of this or a dose of that to make his message more palatable, especially if I am serving up truth to my children.

Is Jesus in the House?

Bill and I attended a conference in inner-city Philadelphia years ago and heard a speaker say something that has stayed deep within me. At that time we were wrestling with how to "do" church: traditional or contemporary, mega or mini, cell groups or congregational. This man's esteem for such things was small. He said that what really mattered was the answer to this question: Is Jesus in the house? So true. I have been in unsightly buildings; heard halting, unprofessional music; listened to unpolished sermons—all while keenly aware that Jesus is "in the house." And I have been in lovely sanctuaries, comfortably ensconced in upholstered theater seats while listening to expertly orchestrated worship music and erudite preaching where Jesus seems all but absent.

As I read the Gospels, I am struck by the magnetism of Jesus. Without any marketing, any frills or freebies, he draws a crowd. And they come to him, often at great personal expense, distance, and even hunger. In Hebrews 1:1–13 the writer compares Jesus, not to anything on earth but to the angels of heaven, and there is no contest! Verse 4 leaves no room for doubt that Jesus "became higher in rank than the angels, just as the name he inherited is superior to theirs" (HCSB). In John 2:1–11, we find Jesus upgrading the house wine at a local wedding reception. In fact, the new wine is so superior that the master of the banquet comments to the bridegroom, "You have kept the fine wine until now" (v. 10 HCSB). When Jesus is present, there is a flavor none of us can manufacture. He takes the most tasteless and transforms it. When he arrives, so does the best.

Thankfully, I am under no pressure to make Christianity taste better for my family. Christianity is Jesus, and he doesn't need my help being attractive to others, my children included. Church, religion, and extraneous rules might have a dull taste; but Jesus, never. Of course we make choices about which church we will attend or which school will educate them wisely and prayerfully. But we don't choose those things frantically or fearfully because our trust is not in church or school to draw our kids to Christ. Youth groups can be healthy, encouraging environments for teenagers, but we know better than to rest our hopes for our children's salvation in them.

Since I don't have to add to or prove the attraction of Jesus to my children, where does that leave me? Praying and staying. Praying that they would "taste and see," and staying in him personally so that I, at least, am filled and satisfied. It is comforting to know that I need only offer him to them; he takes care of the rest. And if they are choosing something else on the menu, it isn't because I've offered them tasteless fare. I can agonize over their choice, but I cannot question the allure of Jesus.

QUESTIONS FOR REFLECTION

1. Where does your trust for your children's salvation lie?
2. Do you recognize the fact that Jesus "tastes" far better than the wine of the world?
3. How can you take some time to acknowledge this openly on a regular basis, as a lifestyle? (It's called worship.)

CHAPTER SIXTEEN
Do They Have a Choice?

One night I was deciphering my son's notes on Genesis for Bible class in an attempt to quiz him for a test the next day. A note in the margin caught my eye: "Love that is not a choice is not love." So I asked him, "Because you are in a Christian home, do you feel loving Jesus is expected of you, and therefore you have no choice in the matter?"

He barely hesitated, "Yes, I do."

This from a young man who does genuinely love Jesus, who is not really rebellious, who gets it. So I began to wonder, *Is it right to believe in, even trust in this formula: Christian home plus Christian youth group plus Christian school equals Christian child?* Can I relax in deterministic bliss, knowing I have made it virtually impossible for my children do anything but surrender to the inevitable?

Formulas and False Security

Formulas make us feel secure. Two plus two is always four, and the day it isn't is the day we expect the world to implode. It is natural to want the equation for raising children to be foolproof, as boringly sure as two plus two equals four. Algebra is almost soothing in its absolute certainty that the number for x is ultimately attainable. Here's an example of a simple formula most of us live by: Me + My seat belt = Relative Driving Safety. We've ingrained that one in our sons. They have even thanked us for instilling the habit in them, thereby literally saving a life on at least one harrowing occasion. In a formulaic vacuum it works like this: Parent's wise counsel + Obedience = Safety.

Two young men in our boys' school were in a tragic auto accident their senior year. The passenger was not wearing a seat belt and was thrown from the car. The driver wore his seat belt. The seat belt wearer was killed, and the young man who was thrown from the vehicle was only slightly injured. My heart hurts over the loss of such a bright star of a young man and for his parents who will never be the same again. My mind wishes for a neat package of safety that could have saved both lives. Now I'm reminded that my own sons are vulnerable. So do I tell them, "There are no guarantees: drive whatever speed, wherever, seat belt or not, and God help you!"? Or do I lock them in their rooms and never let them brave the dangerous highways again? No, I still wear my seat belt and insist they do as well. The safety formula is a good one, but I know we live in a dangerous, flawed world.

At first glance it seems that to throw out the formula means to throw out hope. As my children wade (correction—dive) into independent thinking and acting, I long for secure moorings. And often, the reminder that "faith is the reality of what is hoped for, the proof of what is not seen" (Heb. 11:1 HCSB) presents a problem. While struggling to be certain of an outcome I can't yet see, I am blinded by what I do see clearly—their free will (they had it all along; adolescence and looming adulthood make it louder than life) and my lack of control. But I must reckon with these two facts: my children get to choose, and I can't make them. And, really, if that were not true, two other things could not be true: their ultimate, free choice to love Jesus and his power to love them to the brink of that choice.

What if we've faithfully done the formula? Maybe we haven't done it perfectly, but we've honestly tried. Where does that leave those of us who have yet to see one of our children make the choice to follow Christ? Waiting. Waiting not for the formulas to do their magic but waiting for God—who is more powerful, kind, and loving than we are—to act. Waiting for a miracle, for a dream come true. Most of us don't find waiting comfortable. Even if we're waiting just the space of a short ten minutes, we fidget and fuss, we fill up the time with solitaire on the computer, cleaning out our purse or wallet, inane TV—sounds and stuff.

In Scripture, waiting is neither inane nor idle. Lamentations 3:26 says, "It is *good* to wait quietly for the salvation of the LORD" (NIV). Why is waiting both necessary and difficult? Because we are not God. Solomon, wisest of kings, says it poetically, "God has made everything beautiful for its own time. He has planted eternity in the human heart, but even so, people cannot see the whole scope of God's work from beginning to end" (Eccles. 3:11 NLT). Compared to God's perspective, our view of the future is myopically inadequate. What seems to us like waiting in the dark is just a stroll along a perfectly lighted path to him.

Waiting for the Beauty to Unfold

When I was a little girl, I had a dainty, delicate Japanese fan. Even in its compact form, it was a thing of beauty—exquisite brass trim, satin tassels, a taut accordion of color with the potential to unfold even more beauty. Try as I might, I could never master the coy, Geisha-like snapping open of my fan in one brisk motion. In fact, I tore a few of the creases with the trying. I eventually settled on a slow, gradual unfolding of the design that could mesmerize me for long moments.

It seems my impatience to unfold beauty before its time has followed me into motherhood. My small children were those tightly creased fans—bristling with potential, snug little folds in my palm. I was often too quick to whisk one stage out the door and usher another in. Hurrying through the diaper stage to the potty-training stage or hastening from bicycles to driver's licenses led to a fast-paced approach to things that are supposed to happen slowly. I wanted to see character growth, spiritual sensitivity, and adult-like maturity much more quickly than is fair. The result was impatience and an inability to see the beauty of the process.

As I contemplate the Scriptures, I now notice that most of the promises I cling to regarding my children are in the future tense: "her children *will* rise up and call her blessed" (Prov. 31:28 NKJV, author's italics) "when he is old, he will not depart from it" (Prov. 22:6 KJV) (Wouldn't we all like to know the exact definition of *old*?), or "your sons will be taught of the LORD" (Isa. 54:13 NASB). I've greedily wished for these promises to snap open in my children's lives *right now.* In my impatience I've caused a tear here and there in the creases of their lives. How thankful I am for what Oswald Chambers calls "the magnificent leisure of God." He is "opening" them gradually, revealing a beautiful design. And if I wait and watch, I am mesmerized.

The Design

What is it we wait for in our children's lives? One year my husband gave me a Mother's Day card in which he wrote, "Someday our children will rise up and call you blessed without me telling them to!" It can be gratifying to have a son or daughter, for whom you have sacrificed, grow up to show heartfelt gratitude. I got an e-mail from one of our sons when he had been away at college for about a month. He eloquently poured out his love for us and his gratitude for our spiritual influence in his life, ending with, "I owe so much to you two that I could never repay, but God has your blessings in heaven." No, I got my blessings in that email. I promptly printed and saved it; I would have bronzed it if I could! His gratitude scores big with me. When our children thank us, it is the cherry on our sundae.

Equally satisfying may be those milestones we all celebrate for our children. Graduations from kindergarten, then high school, then college, rank as commemorative destinations in the parenting journey. Our neighbors' yards sprout congratulatory signs in them each spring as graduation dates approach. The signage is getting more and more lavish. I can picture the moms and dads in those homes happily tendering the cash for those signs as they sigh, "Finally!" We've posted two such signs ourselves already—it feels good!

I have a simple prayer for each of our sons, and the answer to that particular prayer is the focal point of all my waiting. "Lord, may Matt, David, Stephen, and Andrew each have a face-to-face encounter with you in which they choose you as their Lord and Savior." I know that the fulfillment of this desire will begin the unfolding of unspeakable beauty. I know that my hopes and dreams for them hinge upon it. I also know that this answer is outside the realm of my control.

And so I wait.

The Posture of Waiting

"I will stand at my watch and station myself on the ramparts. . . . Though it linger, wait for it; it will certainly come and will not delay" (Hab. 2:1, 3 NIV). Here is the voice of a prophet waiting for God to do his thing. Habakkuk's waiting posture is clear. Like him, I can "stand at my watch" and "station myself" as I wait for my prodigal to return. This posture not only implies a graceful, determined anticipation, but also seems to preclude the damage that can be done when we act impatiently. To be standing means to be ready to act, ready to obey. A sitting watchman is not alert and could easily fall asleep! "On the ramparts" means I am securely fortified against assaults from the enemy. "Though it linger," is my perspective. "Will not delay" is God's perspective.

When Habakkuk says, "I will look to see what he will say to me" (v. 1 NIV), the words "to me" literally mean "in me." In other words, he knows that God will speak personally, internally to him. I have discovered that in order for God to speak to me in this way, I must be still and quiet. I can memorize his truth, I can read it, and I can listen to it spoken by those much wiser than I; but when my heart is broken and waiting, I need to hear him speak *within* me. Waiting, as one commentator writes, "with a fixity of attention" affords me the quiet and stillness I desperately need to hear him speak.

What constitutes your "watch"? Do you have a specific place in your home where you pray for your children, where you watch? Maybe your son is literally away from home, and kneeling at his bedside is where you wait. Perhaps you pray in the living room chair that swivels to face the window. Your keen eyes stop from time to time to look for the familiar headlights making their way to your driveway. This is where you take your concerns, the rumors a neighbor shares about your daughter, the next issue you know you need to address. This is where you celebrate the beauty in your son's eyes today, the grace in your daughter's attitude last night, the little sparks of hope that fly from your hearth and warm you as you wait. This is where you cry out, "How long?" and where you ask God, "Why our family?" This is where God reminds you that he is at work and the thing you ask for "will certainly come and will not delay."

This is where the dark path, for a moment, is illuminated. Where "every valley shall be raised up, every mountain and hill made low" (Isa. 40:4 NIV), so that the hope beyond the bend in the road is visible ahead. This is where you wait.

QUESTIONS FOR REFLECTION

1. Have you reckoned with your child's free will?
2. How does trusting God and releasing your own control over your child's choice to trust him find balance in your own heart?
3. How can your watchfulness for God to work affect your prayer life?
4. Do you have "waiting places" in your home? Where are they?

Jerusalem, Jerusalem

"O Jerusalem! Jerusalem. . . . How often I wanted
to gather your children together, as a hen gathers
her chicks under her wings, yet you were not willing."
(Matt. 23:37 HCSB)

You wanted Jerusalem
To nest in your embrace.
I want my kids to be there too.
Wrapped in your strong arms, safe, even snug.

Thank you for the familiar anthropomorphism,
For wearing a hen costume, as it were.
For showing your love to be motherly,
Pure, recognizable.

Our tears seem the same,
Until you ask an infernal why?
"Why do you weep?"
I weep too much for myself.
For my own loss,
My own embarrassment,
My own fear,
My own discomfort.

Refine my love,
And the dross of self spills out.

What kind of hen am I?
A selfish one.
You know that, Lord.
Yet you persist
In exposing me to myself.

The interrogation
Makes me blush.
My love is bared
For what it is:
Human.

My nakedness needs a covering.
Your feathered wings of perfect love
Will do just fine.

"Be gracious to me, O God, be gracious to me, for my soul takes
refuge in You; . . . in the shadow of Your wings."
(Ps. 57:1 NASB)

CHAPTER SEVENTEEN
Which Is It?

A new haircut, no haircut, a redecorated bedroom, weird music, blue nail polish, no nail polish, ear piercing, double ear piercing, triple ear piercing, navel piercing, dreadlocks, hair dye, a tattoo. Choosing Spanish class instead of Latin, choosing the guitar instead of piano, choosing lacrosse instead of cheerleading, changing the spelling of a name. Surely in that list, *something* pushes your buttons. The question is: *in your child*, do those things represent rebellion? Or do they represent healthy, normal nonconformity? Which is it? This is a vital but not so easily answered question.

Perhaps you've felt the sting of others answering for you. We had a friend who was convinced that our son's rebellion was the result of the fact that we let him wear baggy pants. Well, at that time in his life, baggy pants, and a host of other things, *did* symbolize rebellion, but the rebellion is gone, and the baggy pants are still around. The baggy pants were a result, but not a cause, of rebellion. Another friend's son let his curly hair grow to shaggy proportions. He remained barely within the confines of our school's dress code, just barely. When he cut it, other parents were relieved that "his little rebellion was over." What? Did anyone bother to notice what an extremely *good* boy this young man was? Is rebellion defined purely by a haircut? By a desire to be unique, to be one's own person?

We forget just how much our opinions are fashioned by our environment rather than by a biblical, universal sense of right and wrong. It is easier to comply with social norms than it is to be genuinely good, but such an approach is narrow and reduces our world to a small place indeed. We lived in a northern state for over five years. Because we were Southerners, Bill and I wanted to instill the "Yes ma'am, yes sir" habit in our boys. But every time one of them

dutifully uttered one of those ingrained epithets in public, the listener was either offended or confused. We eventually gave up. By
the time we moved back to the South, it was too late to establish the
habit, and by then we had concluded that regional mores were just
that, merely regional. Rudyard Kipling understood well how provincial attitudes can shrink our world. In "We and They," with his
tongue planted firmly in his cheek, he says:

> *All good people agree,*
> *And all good people say,*
> *All nice people like Us, are We*
> *And everyone else is They:*
> *But if you cross over the way,*
> *You may end by (think of it!)*
> *Looking on We*
> *As only a sort of They![7]*

I have a friend who is beautiful by just about any standard. She
is also a certified tomboy. Her mother is a dignified southern
dowager, complete with garden club membership and a closet full of
matching hats, shoes, and even gloves. As a young girl, my friend
was determined to be everything her mother was not. I'm not sure
this was rebellion, at least not at first. We have known each other
since kindergarten, and for as long as I can remember, she has pre-
ferred dungarees over dresses, climbing over curtsying, and running
over reading. She has also just about driven her genteel mother
crazy. I suspect my friend's determination to be her own person—a
decidedly unladylike person—was galvanized by her mother's long,
constant harangues about decorum, but the spark of individuality
was there all along. She grew to adulthood sufficiently feminine to
marry and raise a family of her own. (With one ladylike daughter,
I might add.)

The Need for Discernment

I'm afraid our haste to label anything not like us "rebellion"
would put us in the wrong camp in Jesus' day. I'm sure we would, by
such standards, find John the Baptist's choice of clothing, diet, and
venue signs of rebellion. Obviously his nonconformity to the norms

of the day were rooted in something much more significant than a teenager's innate need to separate somewhat from the adult world, but it seems we neglect to examine the source anyway!

I come from a long line of nonconformists—artists, thinkers, speakers, and writers. My husband says I live with the fear of being ordinary. It stands to reason that at least some of our children would inherit that fear. Coloring outside the lines can be a delightful thing. Famous painted ceilings and exquisite sculptures spring from such souls. A wise friend long ago advised me to relax and let my expressive children be themselves. She didn't qualify that advice with warnings to correct where appropriate because she knew my tendency to overemphasize discipline. When they were young, she helped me walk the tightrope between freedom and rules in my home.

Fueled by true rebellion, outlandish creativity can be unsettling. Perhaps in the more imaginative teenagers it calls more attention to itself than the more stealthy forms of rebellion. Although blue hair may alert us to possible problems (or not!), another child's rebellion at the socially acceptable frat party may be far more dangerous while totally escaping notice. Parents need wisdom to discern which heart condition is driving their own children. One requires celebration, the other care.

I address these thoughts most pointedly to parents of teenagers because in adolescence the urge to be different is the strongest. It is a time when our children seek out identities that make them distinctive. These identities define them. What they wear, the music they enjoy, and the kinds of vehicles they drive are chosen within the confines of the identity they choose. We all know just how these attempts at uniqueness generally pan out. They end up looking, acting, and talking exactly like every other teenager in their particular crowd. So it is a form of self-expression that both disconnects them from us and connects them somewhere else; and, to some degree, it is necessary. Whether we are in the midst of this dilemma or well past it, our children are never going to agree with every one of our values, and we would do well to monitor our responses to them. Young adulthood, while not as combustible as adolescence, is still a time of exploration. Our son may join an opposing political party, our daughter may choose an offensive color scheme, as young parents they may be different from the example we set for them. How we respond to them still requires discernment.

Discerning Love

The thing about discernment is that it is dynamic, not static; there are no clear formulas. Crazy clothing choices may be delightful self-expression in one young girl, while the same clothes spell trouble in another. Discernment sees beyond the clothing, the hair color, and the outspoken "identity;" it sees into the heart. Philippians 1:9–10 says, "And I pray this: that your love will keep on growing in knowledge and every kind of discernment, so that you can determine what really matters and can be pure and blameless in the day of Christ" (HCSB). I have begun to see the nonconformity of my children, not as a cross to bear, but as an invitation to learn deeper love and greater powers of discernment. As I bring this verse to bear upon my life, I am forced to ask myself some pretty pointed questions.

In Paul's estimation, discernment is an outworking of nothing less than love. If I love my child, I will attempt to discover what is best for him or her. Thus I ask myself, *Is his or her self-expression what I would consider best given his or her personality and temperament? Will it harm her or others? Does it either block blessings from or bring benefits to his life?* It might be that this particular question requires consultation. A father who is an executive may truly believe long hair to be a hindrance to the best in his son's life, but the son may choose to be an artist or musician, therefore his success would not be hindered by a long ponytail. For whatever reason, we can be subjective when thinking about our own kids. I have often sought the input of someone I trust whenI don't know how to respond to "coloring outside the lines" choices or behavior. A teacher or mentor who knows me, our family, and especially the son or daughter in question, can be a valuable resource.

Whether I like it or not, I am also compelled to ask myself this: *Am I myself genuinely pure and blameless?* My motives must be pure before I can rightly judge theirs. This is the point to which so much of parenting must return. Me. All I can see is the hurricane named after my child, but God's still, small voice is speaking directly to *me*. I find I am more able to see through the storm if I will approach God in confession, making myself right before him first.

95

In the process of becoming pure, another question I must ask myself is a tough one. *Are my objections to my child's nonconformist behavior based on discerning love, or am I objecting because of my own embarrassment or disappointment?* One day I took two of my small children and a friend's three-year-old to the grocery store. My friend's son chose aisle seven as his stage for a loud, high-pitched screaming fit. As I tried to deal with him, I comforted myself by saying, "At least he isn't my child!" Then it dawned on me that no one else in the store knew that. We are human, and we can't help but be embarrassed by the behavior of our children at times. (Goodness knows we embarrass *them* regularly when they are in middle school.) But our embarrassment is a sorry bottom line. If we have to get past it in order to love, then we must get past it. I honestly believe that the strain to get past my own embarrassment involving my children's choices has been a way for me to choose love for my child over love for the good opinions of others. Which do we care about the most? It is an important question to answer.

When our children choose to be different from us, it can be awkward, uncomfortable, and maybe even painful. Discerning their needs and the most appropriate response is a process most of us would rather avoid, but it takes us through a sifting that is healthy. They are just being themselves, but we are learning to value the things that really matter.

For Discernment

Grant me, O Lord, to know what is worth knowing,
To love what is worth loving,
To praise what delights you most,
To value what is precious in your sight,
To hate what is offensive to you.
Do not let me judge by what I see,
Nor pass sentence according to what I hear,
But to judge rightly between things that differ,
And above all to search out and to do what pleases you,
Through Jesus Christ our Lord.
—Thomas à Kempis (1380–1471)

QUESTIONS FOR REFLECTION

1. What are some choices your son or daughter has made that, while neutral, cause you disappointment, embarrassment, or pain?
2. How do those choices reflect his or her unique personality?
3. What can you do to celebrate the unique identity of your child?
4. How can you practice loving discernment?

CHAPTER EIGHTEEN
Am I Blushing?

Nobody warned me just how embarrassing parenthood would be. There are days when our home feels like the slapstick routine on a vaudeville stage. My kids are a scream, but I'm talking about the stand-up comedy act we parents produce. My husband says, "Marriage will either humble you or harden you." If that's true, then parenting can make your either harried or hysterical! Given the choice, I'd go with the latter.

The embarrassment begins long before your children have any clue what's so funny. If you have a toddler whose voice is high-pitched, loud, and able to carry across three neighborhoods or seven aisles in the grocery store, you have probably already experienced the shame of having some painful truth broadcast in public. A friend of ours is a dentist. Not only has his profession resulted in children with good dental hygiene habits; it has also produced one articulate three-year-old who delighted in greeting strangers with this charming opener: "Hello. Your teeth are brown and need to be cleaned." When he was about four, one of our children got it in his head that anyone he met who might or might not be a Christian should immediately be informed that they could go to hell. This made for uncomfortable plane rides and visits to the neighbors.

Our children also reveal more about us than we'd like. My mother recalls hearing me tell one of my dolls, "I don't care if your arm did fall off, quit your complaining." She wasn't so sure she liked what my words said about her. When you have children, you can't even tell on yourself when you mess up. Before Bill got in the door one evening, he was subjected to a dramatic reenactment of a fender bender (my fault) complete with sound effects. So much for breaking the news to him at the right time. Once I used the word *tit* as one of my last Scrabble turns. I was desperate, and I meant it in the bovine sense. Our boys delighted in telling future guests to our home about the time I spelled out a swear word on the Scrabble board.

And children are insufferable moralists. When our kids were little, *stupid* was an unacceptable word in our house. If one of them overheard me mutter, "Why did I do that? That was stupid!" I was in their doghouse. The fact that I used the word as an adjective to describe myself meant nothing to them. Our behavior, viewed from the lofty aerie of their simple sense of right and wrong, can be indicting indeed.

Allowing Our Children to Tease Us

A long time ago a friend's father, who is very wise, told me that he decided to let his kids tease him. That was a risky decision to make because we all know how easily teasing can deteriorate into disrespect or cruelty, but it was a risk he was willing to make. He has great-grandchildren now, and doesn't regret the years of teasing. I've spent time with this godly, loving family, and they *still* tease him. They also call him "Chief," and he is every bit the name in the family and in their hearts. Our children were young when I first entertained this notion of allowing teasing. Even if I had not decided to emulate my friend's father, I have certainly given my children enough fodder for matricidal merriment. I'm not sure they can help it.

There are several reasons I'm thankful we have allowed a certain amount of child-to-parent teasing in our home. The first is that it parallels a vital element that, unlike teasing, is a must in the atmosphere of any home: confession. Teasing is a poke in the ribs that reminds me I am not perfect. Just because I am the authority doesn't mean I will always be right; letting our sons tease us hints at that truth. Of course we flinch and react, as we should, if the teasing becomes ugly or too close to home. If it hurts, it is no longer good-natured fun. But there is something healthy in a lighthearted look at our own frailties. If my kids see me laughing at myself, perhaps they will learn that admitting failure is not that difficult. I must add, though, that Bill and I try not to tease our children or each other. One evening at dinner our son David made a remark that came out all wrong. I recognized it because I do it all the time, but

I held my tongue. Andrew, five years younger than David, just couldn't pass up the opportunity to take the upper hand. It was gratifying to watch David allow Andrew to poke fun at him. When a seventeen-year-old can laugh at himself, great strides of maturity have been made!

Second, teasing offers a pressure-relief valve. We all make mistakes, and many of those mistakes are actually harmless. Spilled milk is annoying, but it is not the end of the world. Words that come out all wrong can be more easily straightened out with humor than with stern correction. Life is full of enough somber stuff; humor lightens the load. Sarcasm is a different matter. Bill and I decided before we were even married that we would not be sarcastic with each other, but a gentle, self-deprecating approach can provide the comic relief every home needs.

Third, humor is a way to communicate affection. This, I've learned, is so true of boys. Saying "I love you" out loud can be nearly impossible for a teenage boy, but calling your brother a goofy name does it just as effectively for now. This is, again, risky business. What may be affection to one is hurt to another.

Finally, for a moment humor can be a way to reach an unreachable child. In his book, *How to Really Love Your Child*, Ross Campbell mentions what he calls "the resistant child." He refers to this child as one who is often unresponsive to his or her parents' overtures of affection. It is possible to make connections with this child only in certain ways, according to Dr. Campbell. One of those ways is humor: "For instance, a child may be watching television and see a funny scene. At this time parents have the opportunity to make eye contact, physical contact, and focused attention while commenting on the humorous subject. Parents must be quick in doing this because the defenses of a truly resistant child are down only briefly."[8] My experience is that humor with an unresponsive child can often only be experienced on his or her terms, thus allowing that son or daughter to tease me opens up a door that may not open otherwise.

One other consideration is the fluid quality of the emotional climate in our homes. I used to feel that my reactions to our boys' teasing had to be unilaterally consistent. I tried, but I just couldn't do it.

One of them asked me why the same joke could elicit laughter from me one day and tears the next. I responded that I was preparing them for their wives. While discipline and correction, and values and beliefs need to be consistent, feelings are not always the same way. With that thought in mind, we have prohibited them from fat jokes or, for that matter, any jokes using another's physical appearance as material.

The Ill-Fated Frozen Turkey

Even in the worst of times, a dose of laughter can help. A friend's husband wears an obnoxious green button to his cancer treatment appointments that says, "Ain't Dead Yet." I have an uncle who, before he died of multiple sclerosis, spent years in a nursing home. A visit to him promised to be a rip-roaring event. His sense of humor never wavered, and he blessed everyone around him with it. Somehow, amid the pathos of real ordeals with disease, these men found the grace to laugh.

One night I pulled into our driveway with a heavy heart. A friend of mine was ill, and that night I had learned that her illness was terminal. I unlocked the back door and stepped into the den. Home was a refuge I welcomed that night, but I was in for an entirely different sort of evening. Our son David was fifteen at the time and had been out with a neighbor. To make a long story short, his evening involved a ride in the back of a police cruiser and a future court date. By the time I walked through our door, Bill had already plucked David from the police station. I walked in to find him penitently perched on the den sofa, eyes on the carpet, avoiding eye contact with any of us.

Here is the part that was shameful at the time but hilarious to my family now. (I must say, I still remember with embarrassment.) Bill gently related the events of the night to me while our son sat frozen on the sofa. For about thirty minutes I was frozen too. I would like to say that I then calmly discussed everything with Bill and our son; I would like to say I prayed. Although it is not precisely true that I couldn't do those things, it sure felt like it.

I remember watching a film in sixth grade about death. In the film the mother answers the phone, learns her husband has been killed in a car accident, and then calmly takes the roast out of the

101

oven and turns the oven off before going to the hospital. The point was clear: even in dramatically tragic times, we perform the mundane duties of life with a robotic calm that belies the tragic circumstances. Like the mother in the film, I coolly walked to the garage and opened our freezer, and pulled out a frozen turkey I was planning to roast for dinner the next night. I held that turkey in my arms and cried like a baby. *And then I hurled it across the garage.* Thankfully, I throw like a girl, and it didn't hit anything valuable. It was frozen solid and weighed at least eight pounds, so it would have done major damage to our car. Then I grabbed, one by one, the tennis shoes on the shelf by the freezer and threw them each as hard as I could across the garage. That's when I realized the door was open. Matt peered timidly from behind the door and asked, "Mom, are you alright?"

"I'm fine. Just shut the door."

"Mom, you just threw a frozen turkey across the garage. I don't think you're fine."

Believe it or not, I didn't laugh, but I did immediately recognize the futile absurdity of my actions. Since then we have all laughed about that poor turkey. Our son had to do community service, and since he didn't have a driver's license yet, I had to drive him every time. He was genuinely sorry for the thoughtless "fun" he and his friend had had that night. He paid for it in several ways. He learned from it, and he learned that, even in the direst of moments, his parents could react in the wrong way and later laugh at themselves.

QUESTIONS FOR REFLECTION

1. How has humor been a balm in your home?
2. Do you find it difficult to laugh at yourself? Why is that?
3. How can you "lighten up," even in the midst of heavy times?
4. What benefits can you gain from laughter?

CHAPTER NINETEEN
A Calm Moment in the Eye of the Storm

The only thing worse than a dark night of the soul is your *child's* dark night of the soul. You happen to be reading this book, so the odds are you have been where we have been—desperately hurting and wondering where you went wrong, replaying the previous years and hoping to find the flaws in your parenting so you can fix *something* that will make it all better, praying more fervently than you ever have in your life, and even those less comfortable feelings: shame and embarrassment, anger and frustration. Grief. Catapulted into your own dark night of the soul because, after all, that is where your child is, and you cannot help but join him there.

Valentine's Day happened to fall at the crescendo point of our experience with Matt and at probably the toughest week of our family's life. Given the crisis, I assumed my husband and I would cancel our restaurant reservation and stay home. Of course the date would be off. How could we go? We were in mourning.

The morning of February 14, Bill announced, "We're going tonight. Dress up and be ready, and for one hour we *will not* talk about 'you know what.'"

So for one hour amid soft music, candlelight, and good food, we talked about us and our love for each other. And sweated bullets with the effort. We had often prohibited ourselves from talking about the children on dates, but this was different. This was a tiny fraction near impossible, but we did it. And now, several years down the road, I'm amazed by my husband's wisdom and thankful for his resolve.

We chose something vital that night. The simple insistence on an hour of romance spoke something clearly in the midst of our turmoil. We said to the storm, "We are partners in this thing. We will not accuse each other or withdraw from each other. We are lashed to the mast as one. You can rage about us, but you cannot sink us." And it did not.

Horses or Donkeys?

Early in our marriage we were told that wild horses, when attacked by wolves, stand head to head and kick outward at their enemy. However, when wild donkeys are attacked, they stand rear to rear and kick each other! The lesson is pretty clear. Obviously a son on drugs, a pregnant teenage daughter, or a runaway child is bound to place an enormous burden on your marriage. In fact, when Bill and I speak at marriage seminars, we now list "teenagers and other tragedies" as one of the top ten reasons to work hard at building a solid foundation for your marriage. A strong foundation may bear up under the strain, but it will still take a hit. I know I'm telling you to oil your marriage when you have a child who is the proverbial squeaky wheel making a deafening noise in the background of your home, but the preservation of your marriage is worth a few hours of ignoring the squeak. The following thoughts are almost embarrassingly simple suggestions, but they may be the next thing your marriage needs not only to survive the storm but to navigate your ship to calmer waters.

Forgetfulness

It is fairly easy and certainly natural to emulate those wild donkeys. Raising children is about the only job I know of that has a daily, continual potential for mistakes. At the beginning of our first meeting with a family counselor, I asked him to tell us in detail what we did wrong. He asked why I wanted to know. "To avoid doing it again!" was my reply. At the risk of frustrating me, he refused to give me the list I thought I wanted. I realize now that the only thing I would have done with that list would have been to roll it up and swat Bill or myself with it. I would have allowed it to transform me into a wild donkey.

Paul's words in Philippians 3 proved helpful, "But one thing I do: *forgetting what is behind* and reaching forward to what is ahead,

I pursue as my goal the prize promised by God's heavenly call in Christ Jesus" (vv. 13–14 HCSB, author's italics). Not only did I need to forget my own failures and faults as a parent; I needed to forget Bill's. We both are thankful now that we didn't go the route of blaming each other. Talk about adding insult to injury! Of course we have asked forgiveness where wrong, and have sought to change unhealthy habits—that is part of pursuing—but we don't dwell on the mistakes. Not dwelling on them sometimes requires herculean effort, but when we do, the pursuit is made much easier.

For Wives Only

While driving downtown one day, I saw an older gentleman on a bright, shiny, red motorcycle, wearing a bright, shiny, red helmet and an impressive red leather jacket. His white mustache flowed above a self-satisfied grin as he zipped through the light ahead of me. But what caught my attention was the beautiful young blonde (and I mean not-many-years-past-college young) in a matching helmet and jacket holding on for dear life behind him. As I scrutinized them, my feminine intuition told me she was not his daughter. All the way home I mused, *Why is it so many middle-aged men discard the wives who have aged beside them for twenty to thirty years for a trophy wife who is barely old enough to be their daughter?*

The obvious assumption is that the reason is a purely physical, sexual one. These women are perky, beautiful, energetic, thin, and, well, *young.* The first wives are tired, less attractive, distracted, thick, and, well, *old.* Observation has caused me to amend that answer. These young women, because of their daughter-like inexperience, are able to offer older men something men everywhere crave: respect. The trials of life, weariness, or just living for years with an imperfect man can drain wives of their capacity to give that priceless gift to their husbands. Ephesians 5 does not tell us to love our husbands; we are told to respect them. Perhaps that is because respect translates into love in our husbands' hearts. It is all too easy to withhold respect during a crisis involving our children, but to do so would be to rob our husbands of the air they need to stay afloat. Respect is the proactive course to pursue when "forgetting" the mistakes and failures of the past. This is the lion's share of "pursuing." This is what our husbands need most to face the challenges ahead.

Don't Close the Vent

I love reading the Psalms. I'm convinced David was an extrovert who "talked to think" (not an introvert, who would "think to talk"). So many of the Psalms start out with no-holds-barred rage or despair or sorrow. In fact, many of them ramble on in poetic pathos until the end, when David finally affirms that God is God and that his will will, in fact, prevail. Psalm 13 begins with "How long, O LORD?" and ends with "I will sing to the LORD, because He has dealt bountifully with me" (NASB). Psalm 60 starts with, "O God, You have rejected us," and ends with, "Through God we shall do valiantly" (NASB). In Psalm 142, David moans, "I pour out my complaint" in the beginning, only to exude at the end, "For You will deal bountifully with me" (NASB). David knew what it was like to be disinherited by a father figure, to be hunted by his kinsmen, to be resented by his wife. He knew the pain of a mutinous son, and that pain, at times, was an out-loud pain. Sometimes ours is the same. We must speak it or explode! I heard a respected counselor and writer say once that the healthiest people he knows are the people who are able simply to talk to others about their struggles. Our marriages must be the first place we can process pain out loud. I must, for my husband's sake, learn to listen to feelings without reacting, judging, or "fixing."

But marriage cannot be the *only* place to vent. Not too long ago, I for whatever reason, went to bed caught up in a morass of negative emotions. Everything appeared dim and dismal. I instinctively knew (actually, I think it was the Holy Spirit restraining me) that I needed to vent elsewhere. Bill was exhausted, burdened with responsibilities, and it was late with the alarm inexorably set for early. But I spilled my cupful of bitter brew all over him anyway. Pure selfishness. He is the best listener I know, so he absorbed it all bravely, but I awoke knowing the first order of the day was an apology.

Then I went to the Word. Psalms 105 and 106 reminded me to be thankful. Bill could never in a million years have preached to me to give thanks. One night early in our marriage I huffed at him,

"I don't need sermon number 57 right now!" God's Word could preach to me though. Soon I was able to thank God for the things that seemed unbearably onerous the night before.

A mom's prayer group was scheduled for that morning. Each mom walked into my kitchen venting about the same stuff that had laden me the night before. And, interestingly, they thought about those issues in the same way I did. I needed those women; they are my emotional kin. My husband needs for me to have peers who think, fret, and process like I do; otherwise the sheer volumes of words would suffocate him. Same-gender friends provide a pressure-relief valve that brings relief and balance.

The Sixty-Second Hug

One day Bill and I were hugging in the kitchen. Andrew, then five years old, walked through and muttered, "Get a room!" I sure hope he didn't comprehend the meaning of his comment. But the thing is, sometimes you need a physical connection *without* getting a room. In other words, touching outside the bedroom is a way for much-needed healing, intimacy, and support to pass between you. Sandra Anne Taylor, who wrote *Secrets of Attraction: The Universal Laws of Love, Sex and Romance,* offers a scientific explanation we all know is true: "When you touch, your bodies produce oxytocin, which creates a feeling of serenity."[9] An older couple in our church introduced us to the practice of the sixty-second hug. We thought their little habit was a quaint idea, but, feeling ourselves advanced in the area of intimacy, we were sure instituting such a habit in *our* marriage would be like putting training wheels on a Harley. Well, sixty whole seconds of just standing there in an embrace can be a long time. Try it when your day was a killer, dinner is on the stove, children are clamoring for help with homework, and the phone is ringing, and it can seem like compulsory affection, an obligation. But we persisted and have found that those minutes of touch keep us tethered to each other when all of life seems determined to wedge us apart.

Partners for the Long Haul

One of our sons, feeling his father to be injudicious at that moment, asked, "Dad, why do you always side with Mom?"

His wise father replied, "Because you'll be gone in a few years. Mom is going to be around forever!" Not quite true, but the concept is sound. Our time with our children is brief, especially compared with the "till death do us part" timetable of our marriages. In fact, Ecclesiastes 9:9 tells a husband, "The wife God gives you is your reward for all your earthly toil" (NLT). A soul-satisfying, spirit-enhancing, body-thrilling marriage is certainly a proper reward for the "earthly toil" of raising teenagers!

QUESTIONS FOR REFLECTION

1. Perhaps you are straining right now to fully love a child who is resistant or even hostile to you. Can you take a vacation from that effort for a time to focus on loving your spouse in the same intensely committed way?
2. Which of the following do you sense a need for most in your marriage?
   Forgetting
   Opening the Vent
   The Sixty-Second Hug
   Respect
3. What steps can you take to implement a change?

CHAPTER TWENTY
"My Child Would Never . . ."

Remember the "Give it to Mikey; he'll eat anything" cereal commercials? How could you not remember? A commercial so iconoclastic there has even been a remake of it! Our oldest son was a Mikey. He never inspected the contents of the spoon; he just opened up and obediently partook. Not so our friend's daughter, Elise. From day one she made an issue out of eating. If it smelled suspect, looked questionable, or sat next to an offending food, she clamped her jaws shut and refused. Amazingly, she grew with no discernible intake of nutrition.

Bill and I had many a smug comment to offer up about Elise; surely her parents' attempts to feed her weren't consistent or methodical enough. Just look at *our* son, the paragon of child-rearing success. I'm sure our glances to each other across the dinner table communicated to our dear friends. I cringe to think of the "helpful advice" we dished out, with an insufferable certainty that our "wisdom," if heeded, would solve all their problems and "cure" Elise. Thankfully we were knocked from our proud parental perch by that delightful antidote: our second child, who, of course, proved to be a picky eater. And so, just desserts all around, we could do nothing but eat our smug words, every last crumb of them.

Sadly my diet often consists of such words. Parents may be among those most prone to harsh judgment of others. At the risk of being cynical, let's examine a few of the usual suspects:

The Young Parent

Until we get there, we can too easily critique or, worse, condemn the parenting practices of others. Those who don't have teenagers find it comforting to prognosticate, "My children will *never* . . ." They honestly believe *theirs* will be the exception. I don't blame them, do you? Out of context teenagers can seem a scary lot, and that is how we view others' children: out of context. We look at their sullen faces and crazy antics and recoil. It just makes sense to use our words to fend off any possibility that *our* children will travel that road.

The Frightened Parent

This parent senses trouble with her own child and therefore reacts in a panic to any other kid who may seem like a bad influence. Shielding your teenager from the wrong crowd is not a bad idea at all, but it must be done with a sensitivity to the parents of those "wrong crowd" kids. I remember when one boy in our neighborhood was forbidden from spending time with our son. I truly understood, but we didn't need a phone call announcing to all within earshot of our answering machine that we were inadequate parents. Why not a, "How can I help?" message? It wasn't long before our neighbor's son was in his own brand of hot water. The thing about the frightened parents is that often their instincts about their own child are on the money. Prohibited from your son or daughter, their child will just find someone else in the "wrong crowd." We discovered that the old adage "where there's a will there's a way" was stronger than many of the protective measures we took. We controlled where our son was, who he was with, and how much money (almost none) he had, but he still managed to find the lifestyle choices we thought we kept out of his reach.

The Parent in Denial

This parent can't see past the shining perfection of his own child. This is the "young parent" who has never grown out of the "my child would never!" stage. Teachers are well acquainted with this species. A bad grade means poor teaching. A detention means an unfair disciplinary system. Unwilling or unable to face his own child's misbehavior, this parent will most likely lash out at the closest available target: another teenager. Teenagers almost exclusively befriend people like themselves. It may be a rude awakening, but if our kids are choosing the riffraff, it may be because, for now, they *are* the riffraff.

The Wise Parent

I'm not exactly sure how anyone with several teenagers advances to this level. This is the parent who knows it all. I thought that appellation was reserved for the teenagers themselves. This well-meaning parent will quote profusely, give you books and tapes, all with the hidden message that all you need to do to right all your wrongs is heed her advice. They latch onto the newest information offered by the newest parenting guru and are more than willing to pass it along.

The Perfect Parent

Let me say first that these parents don't exist. And if you think they do, put on your red slippers, click your heels together, and go back to Kansas. If such parents did exist, we'd all want to drop a house on them! Although there may be some parents who posture themselves as perfect (see the "Young Parent" above), this is primarily an illusion of our own fashioning. We read a glowing Christmas newsletter, watch our neighbors' children garner award after award, observe the exemplary manners of the Boy Scout down the street, and, in our own sense of failure, neglect to see any of the inevitable faults. Usually these phantom pictures of perfection plague us unnecessarily because the pictures are like still photos rather than the more realistic panorama of a reality video.

Miserable Comforters

These parents dot our landscape and can drop an occasional bomb—in the form of advice—on us when we're down. I recently drove by a vivid picture of how these bombs can make us feel. In the early morning mist, I saw neat stacks of an entire apartment full of someone's belongings lined up on the sidewalk. Urban haystacks,

consisting of beds, a few chairs, and sodden boxes, leaned precari-
ously close to the street. The story behind those mounds of junk was
clear: eviction. Someone's life fallen apart. Later on the same day,
I drove past the same apartment complex and noticed children's
clothing littering the sidewalk. Four or five women were rifling
through the boxes like eager yard sale shoppers. I couldn't help but
think of the young mother whose meager personal effects were being
picked over. There were times when it felt as if our family was
evicted from the ranks of all other Christian families, and our hurt
was spilled out on the sidewalk for all to see. Most walked by and
delicately looked away, but some rummaged, poking around the hurt
and exposing it even more.

Job was a man who understood precisely how it felt for others
to rummage through the ruins of his loss. Look in on an ancient
conversation recorded in the Old Testament. Job has lost just about
everything he holds dear: his land, his wealth, his children, his
health, and comfort. He hasn't lost his wife, but *she* has lost whatever sweetness and faith she had. Her advice to Job is "Curse God
and die" (Job 2:9 NIV). In the midst of his solitary suffering come
Job's friends to comfort him. Job listens politely for a while and
finally laments, "I have heard many things like these; miserable
comforters are you all! Will your long-winded speeches never end?"
(Job 16:2–3 NIV). These advisors ramble on and on, each one sure
he knows the reason for Job's troubles. Each one wraps up the blame
and plunks it pointedly at Job's feet. As a parent you may have been
told by one observer you didn't discipline enough, while another
censures you for being too harsh. You may have a mental log of the
comments by "miserable comforters." Like Job, you listened
politely, but it took you days to recover.

I received a letter not long ago from such a comforter. Years
before, when I needed her friendship, she had judged me as a mother,
and I had allowed her well-meaning comments to fester. I saw the
return address and immediately put up my guard. I expected more of
her advice. But her first sentence made it clear I could let down my
guard. The letter was raw heartache on paper. This friend's daughter
was where our son had been several years before. She wrote to me
because she thought she would find understanding and compassion

from me. Oh, how I hate to report my initial response. As I read her letter, I could not control a subdued grin. I actually found personal satisfaction in her dilemma. I felt vindicated somehow. In my hurt and ultrasensitivity, I had done far worse than she. I had made her my adversary.

Bringing Relief

But that is not what Job did. He recognized the hidden barbs and hurtful implications in his friends' words, and he determined to be a different kind of comforter. In Job 16:5, he vows, "But *my* mouth would encourage you; comfort from *my* lips would bring you relief" (NIV, author's italics). Of all people, I should have sensed my friend's plea for real, substantial comfort. In her eagerness to help me, she had hurt me; but the hurt was largely due to my own tender condition. When we are wounded, especially regarding our children, we are more sensitive to the reactions of those around us.

Unlike Job we can usually relate to the unkind words of others because we have most likely spoken them at one time or another ourselves. But like Job we must commit to speaking words that encourage, comfort, and bring relief. A single-mom friend of mine lives in an apartment with her two sons. She is a great mom, and they are great boys. Her oldest son and another boy got in a fender bender in the apartment complex parking lot not long after they got their driver's licenses. The accident was their fault, the result of typical teenage negligence. This is what the other boy's mom said to my friend; "I knew I should never have let Timothy hang out with *your* son. And especially not in an *apartment*."

The implications don't need to be spelled out. The words of a frightened parent translated into an attack on my friend's character and her home. I can relate to both moms. I have said things to other parents that have hurt them. I have been hurt as well. The day my friend vented her pain to me, I decided that a blanket apology was in order. I wrote the following as an injured cry and a confession all in one. I wrote it for all parents. Perhaps it is the medicine we all need.

My Apologies . . .

For saying, "My child would never . . ."
For labeling your son a "bad kid" based purely on secondhand information, an isolated incident, or appearance alone.
For rolling my eyes in a knowing way when your daughter is mentioned.
For making light of what is burdening you.
For making hurtful assumptions: that your home is defective in some way, that your circumstances are your fault, that I could raise your children so much better than you could.
For not bothering to offer my help, not bothering to pray.
For feeling smug that my kids are on the right track.
For assuming your child influenced mine; mine is not responsible.
For not looking into the face of your child and choosing to love or understand.
For choosing the world's way when Christ's way is my mandate.
For these failings that have hurt you, I ask forgiveness.

And, in an effort to repent, I commit to . . .
Tread carefully.
Speak charitably.
Act delicately.
And pray mightily.

QUESTIONS FOR REFLECTION

1. When have you been a "miserable comforter," quick to place blame on a hurting parent's shoulders?
2. When have you been hurt by such a comforter?
3. How can you take steps to become the kind of comforter Job desired to be?
4. Do you know a parent who needs you? Take a few moments to begin praying for that parent and for an opportunity to offer him or her some relief.

I Still Love You

O Lord,
If the promises I read in your Word
Are true
(This if revealing
The still-tentative nature
Of my faith),
If . . .
Then I
Tremblingly,
Expectantly,
Respectfully,
Ask you to
Prove it.

There are people in my heart
Who are asking if
(This if revealing pain,
A tentative trust,
Or even mocking),
If . . .
This mighty God
Still has his might.
And I am
Wanting a dose
Of such knowledge, too.

But,
I want you to know:
If you linger
In your silent If
(This if reveals my
Tentative peace
With your sovereignty),
Well, I
Still love you.

CHAPTER TWENTY-ONE

A Remembered Conversation

One fine spring day during my freshman year in college, I got a call from my high school youth pastor. He and his wife were in town. Could they come by this afternoon for a visit? Bob and Becky and their three daughters met me later that day in the lobby of my dorm. Two of the girls were ensconced in their strollers, and Amy, the oldest at only four, held onto her mother's legs. Becky was a conscientious mom and had everything needed to occupy the girls for at least an hour's visit. We made the short walk to the outdoor amphitheater on campus and settled on some mossy stone steps in the shade.

Less than one year earlier I would have called Becky one of my most esteemed role models. She was vivacious, kind, and wise. She was a great mom and wife. But now I was a know-it-all college freshman. Two and a half quarters at a forward-thinking women's college had rendered me insufferably full of myself. I was proud of my academic achievements and the ambitious plans I had laid out for my life. Of course it didn't occur to me, as I regaled them with my proposed double major, that one of Becky's great disappointments had been the interruption of her college career. Several years later I recalled our conversation that day and remembered Becky's one comment to me. She gestured proudly toward her daughters and said, "Here are my diplomas. I can't frame them or hang them on my wall, but I'm proud of them."

She said it a little wistfully but not regretfully. I remember my response with great dismay now. I recall that my face wrinkled into a grimace as I ejaculated, "Oh, I don't want that kind of diploma! I have more ambition than that."

It's amazing how clear the reception can be on the screen of a memory we wish we could rewind and play over again. Becky didn't respond to me verbally, but I can still see the hurt expression on her face. By the time I grew up enough to rue my hasty words, I had lost touch with Becky and Bob.

His Creation, Not Ours

Like most wisdom we gain from a human messenger, the truth in Becky's comment was flawed. Or my understanding of it was flawed. Or both. One thing was true: children, family, and the role of parenthood are all vastly more valuable than any academic achievement we might gain. By the time I had children of my own, the diploma I had so prized was gathering dust in a box in the attic. My GRE score means nothing to me now. I care much more about the Friday spelling test my son has to take each week. Becky knew the value of her "diploma" and rested in it while I blew the hot air of self-important youth.

Somewhere during our second year of marriage, I began to elevate the parenting of children to this much higher view. By our third year I held our first son in my arms and didn't doubt for a moment that parenting was a supreme calling. The Scripture calls our children arrows in our quivers or olive plants in our gardens (Pss. 127:4–5; 128:3). This would lead us to believe that they are an effect to our cause. But the idea conveyed by a quiver full of arrows or young olive plants is one of blessing, not remuneration. I believe this is a nuance that we would do well to understand. It is a vital subtlety of parenting.

Perhaps the fact that we are made in the image of a Creator God causes us to see our children as our own creations, much as a painter or sculptor esteems the work of art he envisions and crafts with his own hands. Before we leave the hospital, we report to others the resemblances: my nose, his hands, my eyes, grandmother's complexion, grandfather's eyebrows. We are fascinated by this tiny, delicate replica of ourselves. It is all too easy to make the jump in our thinking from, "This child is like me," to "This child *is* me." The latter way of thinking is never conscious, but it leads us to wear our children like badges, to feel that everything they say, do, or even think is a direct result of something we say, do, or think.

It might help us to consider the way God created Eve. He used Adam's rib, thus making Eve similar to him in many ways. But the differences between them were obvious. Adam was a mere contribution to the process, and a contributor who was asleep throughout the whole thing at that! The short, ruinous history of Eden convinces us that Eve had a mind of her own. In the same way our children are like us, but they are not merely an extension of us.

The Fruit of Our Labor

This may seem like mere semantics. I would have said so during those years when our children's minds seemed malleable and their behavior manageable. One morning during a tough time, I read this familiar verse in Luke 6: "A good tree can't produce bad fruit, and a bad tree can't produce good fruit" (v. 43 NLT). Sometimes we can read the right words and think the wrong thoughts about them. That's what I did that morning. My inner translator instantly converted the verse to: "If your children are exhibiting really 'bad' behavior, then it means you are a really bad tree." It's hard to continue reading Scripture when it busts your chops so thoroughly. But suddenly I felt I needed to know from the Lord whether this indictment was true. I backtracked and reread the entire chapter. Interestingly, the "good tree, bad tree" verses follow closely on the heels of another familiar passage, one that commands us not to judge one another. That gave me a glimmer of hope that the purpose of these verses was not solely to grind me into the dust of condemnation.

In order to understand the passage, the question I needed to answer was this: What is the definition of *fruit*? I believe a solid definition can be drawn directly from the passage. According to Luke 6:43–45, the good fruit that grows on a good tree is this:

- Good deeds—In other words, things that I do that are good.
- A good heart—My motives.
- Good words—Whatever is in your heart determines what you say.

This definition has absolutely nothing to do with the actions, motives, or words of any other but myself. That morning I drew this conclusion: *The fruit of my life consists of the things I alone can control and choose. I can choose my actions, the condition of my heart, and my words. I cannot control the actions, the condition of the heart, or the words—the fruit—in the lives of any other person, my children included.*

There are several reasons we shy away from the above conclusion. One is that we still hope to control the fruit of our children's lives, or maybe they are young enough or compliant enough for it to appear that we can. Maybe they are breaking our hearts, and we can't let go of the hope that we can. Another reason is that we have built our little empire around the belief that our children are us. They are so much a part of our identity, our hope, and our world that we can't let go. Finally, if we believe that our own fruit refers solely to *us,* we will have to endure the laserlike inspection of the Holy Spirit deep within, and that is a scary proposition to us. Once I understood the real meaning of the verses in Luke 6, I had to face the words of Jesus in yet another way.

Goals and Desires

Let me see if I can say this another way. A distinction we must make as parents is the distinction between our goals and our desires. Our goals, like our fruit, are the things we can control. Our desires are the things we wish for but cannot necessarily bring about. Let's say I want to have a healthy, intimate marriage. That is a good thing, but it is a desire, not a goal, since I cannot make it happen by myself. What I can control is the kind of wife I am. I can have goals which ultimately contribute to that desire. I can make it my goal to be submissive, a helper, a good listener. All of these are goals I can choose. Thankfully I have a husband who has similar goals for himself and desires for our marriage.

How does this apply to parenting? If we have adult children, the application is easier because they are not around for us to control. I can have goals related to my own behavior. I can decide that I will not criticize or nag. But I must understand that the hope for my adult child's success, for his relationships, for her career are *desires* and should be treated as such. Even parents of toddlers can exercise this subtle shift in their approach. My goal as a young parent can be to discipline in a certain way, to express love in the ways my children need, to provide an atmosphere that encourages obedience, growth, and security. But my child's response to my parenting is a desire not a goal. Each child is different, so my goals for myself as that child's parent may have to be altered accordingly. Again, while this may seem like a complicated word game, the freedom it brings can be astounding.

The week our son Matt was in the hospital we received lots of encouraging mail. At least that was the intent of the senders. It wasn't until later that we could read our mail with any attention to the words. One of the letters I have kept is from a couple in my hometown. Their daughter and I had been friends for over thirty years. I respected them as parents. I knew that two of their sons had battled drug or alcohol addiction in their early adult years, but I had never talked with them about it. Their letter, all four pages of it, is still a valuable resource for me. One short sentence sums up the change in thinking that is so vital, yet so difficult, for us to make: "When we finally realized we were powerless, we received peace, and God brought [our sons] to the end of themselves." At the time, that last phrase was foreign to me. To admit powerlessness was to admit defeat, or so I thought. The truth is, I *am* powerless over the fulfill-ment of my desires in other's lives. Facing that raw reality leaves what power I do have fully available to me to pursue the goals I can actually achieve as a parent.

The line between your goals and desires as a parent may have been blurred for so long that you may think it is too late to revamp your thinking. Your child may be so steeped in addiction, sin, or rebellion that you don't have the mental energy to tackle something as subtle as a paradigm shift. You might find it helpful to ask the goal/desire question as you pray, or, if your children are young enough to be around, when you interact with them. Another way to look at this may be through the eyes of a farmer. A down-to-earth friend of ours once commented, "I can keep my row pretty straight as long as I look at it while I hoe. But if I look over at another person's row while I'm hoeing, mine gets crooked." It may be that our goals are neglected or become crooked when all our focus is on the changes we wish to see in our children's lives. What our kids need most is parents who hoe straight rows themselves.

QUESTIONS FOR REFLECTION

1. How have you viewed your children as an extension of yourself?

2. What are your personal goals as a parent?

3. What are your desires for your children?

4. How can you make the distinction between the two clearer? Why is that necessary?

CHAPTER TWENTY-TWO

Squirming in Sunday School

The fact that midlife and the end of the hands-on phase of parenting fall at approximately the same time in our lives can seem like a cheap trick at times. One spring Sunday morning I sat in a classroom full of young couples and watched a videotape telling us how to instruct our children about the godly use of money. With the exception of the teacher and his wife, I had four children and at least twenty years on every other person in the room. What sounded new, challenging, and exciting to them fell on my ears like stinging accusations. Sure, Bill and I instructed our children about money, and sure, we implemented many of the principles presented on the video, but looking back (seems I do that a lot these days), I couldn't help but feel the weight of all that we *didn't* do.

Here's the dilemma in which I found myself on that Sunday morning: do I respond to God's Holy Word and the wise counsel of others with a cynical, "Ha! Yeah right! Been there, done that, and it isn't as cut-and-dried as you make it sound." Or do I melt into a pitiful puddle in my chair and consider myself an utter failure, really not qualified to call myself a parent at all? The former is the pathogenesis of bitterness and the latter of despair. Neither sounds inviting, do they? Not to me they don't, but I often allow myself to be the rope in that tug-of-war.

As the credits rolled, our teacher clicked off the video and looked at us with a wry grin. He and his wife have raised three godly, responsible children. Not only that, he is an accountant, so I sat like a deer in the headlights, poised to flinch at the good advice he might offer that would only add to the list of indictments against me. He shared with us that he had previewed the video the night before while monitoring the progress of the war in Iraq on his television. He said, "As I compared the neatly packaged instruction in the video to the messy war statistics I watched before and after, I couldn't help but think, *Here is the perfect life we all desire, and here is real life: war.*"

I could have kissed him! The tension that had stretched to an unbearable tautness in my soul relaxed. Our teacher recognized something I often forget to acknowledge: Life this side of heaven is full of such tensions.

Living with the Tensions

If I follow Jesus, I must face the tensions. I will struggle between the Spirit and my flesh, the reality that I live in this world and the desire not to be of it, the balancing act of mercy and justice. Don't want to face the tensions? Just observe entire communities of Christians who have opted for the safer extremes: the legalists and those who live licentiously, the hermits retreating to their caves and those who become so immersed in popular culture they have no distinctively Christian identity, the impoverished ascetics and the "health, wealth, and prosperity" preachers of today.

These tensions are sharpest for me as a parent. How can four human beings produce in me both ecstatic musing and existential malaise? How can I vacillate daily between regretful retrospection and sweet sentimentality? How can I find them both appealing and appalling all in the same day? How can I envision one as president of the United States one day and a derelict on skid row the next?

And then there's my own competence as a mother. How can I trust God implicitly for my children's welfare one moment and wallow in worry the next? How can I berate myself for being too lenient today when yesterday I feared I was too harsh? My own self-doubts inflict grave damage to my efforts at consistency. When I spend time now with young, hopeful parents, I find I envy their wide-eyed innocence. I wish for the days when a videotaped instruction gave me nothing but encouragement to press on and produce near-perfect kids.

Perhaps the most frustrating tension I experience is the confusion that occurs when I observe other mothers and wonder, *Are they doing it right while I am doing it all wrong?* And when I have a child who disobeys or strays, I languish in the tension even more. Take my friend Heidi; she and I cannot be more opposite in our approach to mothering. She is extremely structured; I'm not. She disciplines differently. One of us homeschools; the other does Christian school. She never opens a package of processed food to feed her family; I've made peace with boxed macaroni and cheese for lunch. The list goes on. At times the tension between us, at least in my own mind, is palpable.

The Though and the Yet

The tensions within us and between ourselves and others are not the only tensions we feel. Sometimes the encouraging promises in God's Word, juxtaposed to our current experience, seem almost fantastical. I hate to say that the Scripture reads like false advertising, but it can feel that way. I think the prophet Habakkuk knew this particular tension. In chapter 3, perilous realities and prophetic promises strain against each other on the page. In verse 17 he describes the raw realities of his experience as the "though" aspects of his life. "*Though* the fig tree does not bud and there are no grapes on the vines, *though* the olive crop fails and the fields produce no food, *though* there are no sheep in the pen and no cattle in the stalls" (NIV, author's italics). Translated into the culture of Habakkuk's day, this meant there was virtually no fruit, no meat, no wine or milk, no fuel for light or heat, no medicine, no food, no commerce, no jobs, no cosmetics, no new clothing, plus any other commodities, sheep, cattle, olives, and figs produced for the people of his day. Add to this devastation a prophecy of impending invasion that produced fear in the people so thoroughly that Habakkuk said, "I heard and my inward parts trembled, at the sound my lips quivered. Decay enters my bones, and in my place I tremble" (v. 16 NASB).

Verse 18 begins with the only word able to connect our "thoughs" with the real hope of Scripture: "yet." Habakkuk does not stick his head in the sand and refuse to admit that the circumstances are dire, neither does he take up the cynic's poison pen to write his commentary. He takes due note of the realities, some self-inflicted by the people of God and others seemingly haphazard, and courageously utters that all-important "yet":

"Yet will I rejoice in the LORD, I will be joyful in God my Savior" (NIV).

Like Habakkuk, I struggle to accept present realities while affirming permanent truth. It has taken some bootstrap pulling, but I have composed my own "Though . . . yet" verses on various occasions over the years. I have a friend who was impressed by the Lord to write a song based on these verses. Her "though" was the inability to bear children. One couple battled for years with near ruin financially, and that is their "though." Another friend's "though" is the pain of divorce, while a single friend's "though" is her singleness. As parents, our "though" can be strongest during the hard times with a rebellious or hurting child. During the "though," how can we accomplish the liberating proclamation of a "yet"? There is only one way. The last verse in Habakkuk says, "The Sovereign LORD is my strength; he makes my feet like the feet of a deer, he enables me to go on the heights" (NIV). The choice to praise God is a trip to "the heights" accomplished only by the strength of our Sovereign Lord.

Here is an example of my "though" and "yet" one day:

Oh Lord,
Though I wanted to send Stephen and Andrew to summer
camp,
And though I feel inadequate as a parent because we can't.

And though I feel out of touch with Matt and
Though I feel helpless to close the gap.
And though David's car needs work
And all the boys need new spring clothes
And though I am discouraged about these things and more,

Yet I will sing praises to you today.
You are our Provider in every way
And you are the Provider God,
Jehovah Jireh for our sons as well.

I will choose joy in you today,
And I will rejoice in the things about you, my God,
That are true and never, ever change.

My Presence Will Go with You

Did praise change my circumstances? No, not immediately. But praise, chosen when it is most difficult to do so, can be a reminder that Someone else is in those circumstances with me. One day I was thinking about the differences between my friend Heidi and me, trying to sort through them. As I pondered the tension between us, my mind eventually painted a telling tableau. I pictured Jesus, clipboard in hand, pencil behind his ear, inspecting Heidi's home. He then visited mine with the same clipboard and pencil. Just before I nervously formed the question, "Which one of us passed?" I realized the absurdity of my picture.

I am certain that if Jesus appeared in Heidi's home, she would immediately fall prostrate before him in humility. She would not be able to help it. And the same would happen in my home. As I pondered this scene, the phrase, "The ground is level at the foot of the cross," took on a whole new meaning for me. So that is where the tension is resolved: in the presence of Jesus. Ultimately heaven will dissolve all tensions, but for now the extent to which I live in his presence is the extent to which the tensions will fade. Not completely, but their ability to distract and annoy and confuse will dissipate.

It is his presence that gives me the strength I need to say, "Yet will I rejoice," when the tension between his standards and my reality, his promises and my experience, becomes too much. And it is his presence that neutralizes the tensions that inevitably arise between his people. Moses knew just how desperately he needed the presence of God in his own life. In Exodus 33, there is a conversation among God and Moses which begins with God's promise, "My Presence will go with you, and I will give you rest" (v. 14 NIV). Although God has just promised to be with him, Moses asks for a confirmation by saying, "If your Presence does not go with us, do not send us up from here" (v. 15 NIV). It is the tensions in life that cause me to beg, as

Moses did, for the same confirmation. "Lord, if you don't go with me out into this unsettled world of parenting and just plain living, don't send me out there!" Thankfully, God, who was not obliged to, left heaven in order to do just that. As I soak in that fact, the tensions relax, and I can do the very thing he has on his heart for each of us to do: "Be still before the LORD, all mankind, because he has roused himself from his holy dwelling" (Zech. 2:13 NIV).

QUESTIONS FOR REFLECTION

1. What tensions have you experienced as a Christian?
2. What tensions have you experienced as a parent?
3. What are the "thoughs" in your life right now?
4. How can you say a "yet" of praise to the Lord?
5. How can you experience God's presence in your life more fully?

CHAPTER TWENTY-THREE

Hanging Out
with Superstars

Our son Stephen plays on two soccer teams every fall. On one team he gets to shine. He is one of the better players, and for most of the other guys he raises the bar. They follow his example and look to him for their cues. He usually wins an award at the end of the season. On the other team he has never won an award; he is only one of a squad full of stars. He has no special status. The first team is made up of his friends at school, and the second is a group connected only by their age and skill. I assumed he would prefer the team that allows him to be the best among his peers, but I was wrong. The latter team is the one he can't wait for each fall. Why? Because he would rather be challenged than coddled. At first he felt a little intimidated by these boys until he learned to capitalize on their proficiency. Their superior skill serves to draw a better performance out of Stephen. He wouldn't miss such an opportunity for anything.

I appreciate his example. It is so easy, in every area of life, to "go low," to avoid encounters with people who challenge us to a higher level. One way I have found to rub shoulders with better "players," with the all-stars, is to read the writings and prayers of the ancient saints. Hanging out with these godly men and women has, at times, made me uncomfortable. Read the following two prayers, and the contrast will make it clear why. Ultimately, superstars like Ignatius Loyala, and a host of others, have challenged me to grow.

For Dedication to God

Teach us, Lord,
To serve you as you deserve,
To give and not to count the cost,
To fight and not to heed the wounds,
To toil and not to seek for rest,
To labour and not to ask for any reward
Save that of knowing that we do your will.
                    —Ignatius Loyala (1491–1556)

For Blessings from God

O Lord,
I ask you to serve me today.
I will need a parking space downtown,
You know how hard they are to find.
May the children cooperate today.
I ask you to keep them from harm,
And may they excel in their schoolwork today.
May all our activities "work out" for our good.
And, Lord, may I have peace.
                    —A Believer (21st century)

At first glance these prayers are at the opposite poles of big and small, God centered and self-centered, noble and petty, courageous and cowardly. While the second prayer is a fabrication—I was too embarrassed to quote an actual entry from my own prayer journal— I dare say there are times when we identify more readily with our twenty-first-century brethren who pray such small prayers than with the saints of antiquity whose prayers have endured to challenge us today.

The Great Cloud of Witnesses

It is this contrast that has encouraged me to read the prayers of the saints over the years. They beckon me to the high road. At the very least, they cause me to stop, take stock, and notice that I am on a low road indeed. I meet regularly for prayer with a small group of women. Their lives challenge and comfort me. But they, like me, can so easily become focused on the small things of life. I'm thankful for them and for the fact that God meets us in those small things, but I desperately need the fellowship of "a large cloud of witnesses" mentioned in Hebrews 12:1, who have prayed in faith through the centuries. Therefore I meet regularly with Thomas à Kempis, Martin Luther, Brother Lawrence, Augustine, and Teresa of Avila. Of course I keep company with Moses, David, and Paul as well. I peer into their prayer lives and never fail to come away lifted in my own.

Early one Saturday morning I read Psalm 66. I had started the morning praying over a list that included car repair, travel safety for one of our boys who was returning that day from college, a few specific financial needs, soccer tryouts, and a scheduling snafu that was troubling me. A laundry list of *me, my,* and *I*. As I read, I could not help but notice the startlingly different pronouns in the psalmist's praise:

Psalm 66:2–4 NLT

Sing about the glory of his name.
Tell the world how glorious he is.
Say to God, "How awesome are your deeds!
Your enemies cringe before your mighty power.
Everything on earth will worship you,
They will sing your praises,
Shouting your name in glorious song."

Next I read from a compilation of ancient prayers a friend sent our way. I read prayer after prayer and ended with this humble request by Thomas Aquinas:

A Steadfast Heart

Give me, O Lord, a steadfast heart,
Which no unworthy affection may drag downwards;
Give me an unconquered heart,
Which no tribulation can wear out;
Give me an upright heart,
Which no unworthy purpose may tempt aside.

Bestow on me also, O Lord my God,
Understanding to know you,
Diligence to seek you,
Wisdom to find you,
And a faithfulness that may finally embrace you,
Through Jesus Christ our Lord, Amen.
                    —Thomas Aquinas (1225–1274)

Perhaps Thomas Aquinas prayed also for the minutiae of his life. He was celibate, so the fact that he didn't have a wife or children might have reduced the particulars somewhat, but I'm sure he dutifully offered up the daily details of his life to the Lord. Still, it is clear that his primary prayer focus was much larger than mine. My journal entry for that Saturday read:

O Lord,
Today I'm reading
The prayers of the great saints—
Men and women marking history
For your kingdom.
And then
I glance at my own prayers—
Written by my small heart
And I am so ashamed.
When did I become
So self-absorbed,
So provincial,
So whiny,
So petty?

O Lord,
May I spend my precious
Slice of time with you
Enlarging my eyes
Retooling my purpose,
Stretching my heart
To fit, or more nearly fit,
Yours.

May I walk in
Your opportunities,
Your stride,
Your energy and power,
Your love.

And may I be more riveted to you.
May I please you,
Honor you,
Be found in you.
Amen.

Beyond Praying

I have a friend who made a big transition in her life. She moved from one coast to the other and left a rich support group of friends in doing so. She had to raise the funds for the ministry she was joining. She was single, so all the moving details lay upon her shoulders alone. We met one day before her move, and I asked her how I could pray for her. Her answer astounded me. She said she had made the decision that her prayer life would revolve around the work of the kingdom. She had made a once-for-all petition to the Lord for her personal needs and determined that, because he was committed to meeting her every need, she could move on and devote her prayers to things larger than her needs for housing, transportation, funds, etc. She asked me to pray that God would prepare the way for his work, that he would be honored by her labor, and that people would come to know Christ as a result.

While I believe it is certainly acceptable to pray for every little need we have, I am challenged by my friend's example to pray what I have come to call "beyond" prayers. "Beyond" prayers acknowledge that God is about something much larger in scope than the meeting of a particular need. They recognize that the target is not our own comfort or rescue, but the ultimate goal the psalmist had: that "everything on earth will worship you." They expand my prayers from a thing to "everything" and my vision from my small world to the far reaches of all the earth. This way of praying also readies me for God to work in my life. Charles Hadden Spurgeon said, "If God means to bless you greatly, He will make you pray greatly."

The choice to pray bigger prayers for my children has, for me, been a form of surrender. When I pray for a good grade on a test, I subject my appeal to this larger view. The grade then becomes a dispensable request in the light of God's bigger purpose. I offer up the small need, knowing that a big God might answer differently in order to achieve a higher purpose. That purpose may include the character growth of my child, or it may stretch to include the people God puts in his path down the road. I have to admit that a disappointment may go further in making my son or daughter meet for ministry than one answer to a little prayer. Because I cannot always see what God is about when I look "beyond" in prayer, it makes prayer a bit more of a free-fall sensation. I must trust that God, if he chooses to sacrifice a small thing in my child's life, does not do so without good reason. And I must embrace that reason without knowing exactly what it is.

"Beyond" praying is also a privilege. I am partnering with God himself when I acknowledge and even welcome his purpose in my specific prayers. I am in effect saying to him, "Your will be done," not as a resigned moan but as a resounding mandate. I can then look at my list of prayer requests for my children and feel a certain kind of pride that the God of the universe is crafting his bigger will by addressing those smaller needs in his way.

The problem is that life is full of little things. We live with cars that need repair, tests to be studied for, lawns that need to be mowed, aches and pains that beg for healing, tuition and bills that need payment, and petty conflicts that require resolution. We would do well to pray about those little things. But we would do better to pray beyond them as well. Praying in this way enables us to see the dark times in our children's lives in a new light. It transforms tunnel vision into the broad daylight of God's highest purposes.

QUESTIONS FOR REFLECTION

1. Why do we gravitate to small praying?
2. How would you characterize your prayer life? Your prayers for your children?
3. In what ways can you begin to pray "beyond" prayers?

CHAPTER TWENTY-FOUR
A History Lesson

I was not a history major in college. For good reason. I cannot remember dates and events, at least not in any accurate order. I have a savant friend who remembers minutiae exactly where it fell on the calendar. Pick a date, and she can quickly reference what happened on that date thirteen years ago. On my last visit to the doctor, he asked me, taking notice of my age, if I had "Teflon brain" yet. In other words, nothing sticks. I think I was born with Teflon brain! The advent of my mid-forties has sprayed an extra coat of nonstick spray on the slippery skillet of my brain. I barely remember last week, much less the century in which Attila the Hun lived.

In my quest to have some grip on historical events, I have discovered a tool that helps me look back with some sense of order. The time line. That visual aid can present an entire era in such broad strokes that even my brain can absorb it. The pharaohs parade from pillar to pyramid in perfect order, or the monarchs of England march merrily from the Saxons to the Plantagenants to the Stuarts. History sweeps by leaving an imprint where dry details from the textbooks have glanced off again and again. I especially like the glossy, oversized, pop-up varieties of the time line. No matter that I usually have to find them in the juvenile literature section of the bookstore. The more visual hooks the data has, the better.

The Bible is the same way. Hand me a list of facts, dates, kings, and prophets, and I'm lost. Put it all on a slick, colorful time line, and I get it. Perhaps it is the way the big picture pops out that makes a time line so appealing. My study Bible shows me diagrams of the Israelites' circuitous march from Egypt to the promised land, a sweeping scene-by-scene account of the life and ministry of Jesus, a time-lined travelogue of Paul's journeys. This way I step back to view a panorama that makes sense to me.

What if I looked at how God's children appear *as children* in the Old Testament? I know the people in the Bible were real, grown-up people, but it provides fresh insight if I view their history in a personal way. Like the rungs up the tree trunk of a nursery growth chart, these children grow up as the pages turn. Try this progression of God's people across the pages of Scripture on for size:

Genesis–Joshua

God's children are infants whose first word is no!

Judges–Ruth

The people of Israel are toddlers whose hands are repeatedly spanked.

1 Samuel—Song of Solomon

They are adolescents with all the attendant foolhardiness, angst, and high drama.

Isaiah–Malachi

On the cusp of adulthood, God's people are brash, independent, and self-reliant.

The New Covenant

God's people have grown up. They are now peers. Jesus calls them his friends.

Of course there must be scattered throughout this broad landscape the occasional child who quietly stands above the rest and incurs the wrath of his peers for his trouble. Hebrews 11 lists quite a few of those: men and women who were misunderstood by their underdeveloped, immature fellows, whose lives were used by God to press his people on toward the next stage of their development.

The Wide-Angle Lens

A gaze from this wide-angle perspective reveals two things. First, in this big picture I see God as a timeless Father, rearing his children across the ages. He can identify with me as a parent in each and every stage of my child's life. He knows the joys of an infant's smile and the sorrows of a teenager's hostility. He has been told no, and he has watched his children make mistakes. He has punished in humane, creative, and wise ways. He has waited up for the errant adolescent. He has let go only to watch his children fail. He has also known the button-bursting pride of saying to a son or daughter, "Well done." He has been there in a way my mind cannot fathom. I can trust him to identify with me throughout the twists and turns of my own family's time line. He knows.

As I look across the vast and varied landscape of Scripture, I also see that my Father God is millennially patient. What I would attempt (and fail) to correct overnight, he allows to marinate and eventually change over the course of centuries. This is a regular source of comfort for me. I have a strong tendency to freeze time and view things only in that frozen frame. I then draw conclusions and map out plans based on the miniscule dot of that day or that moment. When it comes to my children, it looks something like this: a poor grade on a test can quickly have the emotional impact of three years' worth of bad report cards. *Oh no,* I think, *my child is a failure at school.* This then leads to what my family fondly calls "machine gun mode": Let's make a plan, call a tutor, stop what we're doing, and all panic together. Maybe I've overstated it. Maybe I don't verbally express any of this, but I certainly feel it. The unfurling history of the Word of God helps me step back and look through the wide-angle lens at my own life. It gives me a big picture when my own small one looks dim or discouraging.

Not only do my children benefit when I zoom out to look at life, but I have a better view of myself when I broaden the horizon as well. One day I read Proverbs 31 through this wider lens. For the first time I was not overwhelmed or intimidated by that confounded virtuous woman. I realized that the account on the page was a retrospective of an entire life's work rather than a time record of one day or even one week. When I considered her many superwoman achievements and wonder woman qualities in this light, she wasn't such an impossible role model to follow. I didn't measure my day against hers (where did she get all those extra hours?). I could follow her and actually hope to be like her. Just give me time.

Personal Time Lines

When I was growing up, my maternal grandparents were very much a part of my life. Holidays not only included them; they were defined by them. I was the oldest grandchild, so I observed the growth of our family events from small, intimate affairs to much larger productions. Thanksgiving and Christmas always found the Burton clan gathered together in my grandparents' gracious home. I remember when my grandmother decided it was time to dispense with the children's table and include everyone at one dinner table. In order to seat us all together, an old green Ping-Pong table was pressed into service and set up in the den, the largest room in the house. No one but my grandmother could have pulled off the transformation from sagging splintered table to banquet deluxe. I don't know where she found tablecloths wide enough to fit or centerpieces with the right proportions, but she did.

I remember the last Thanksgiving we all celebrated around that table before my grandfather died. As was our custom, we passed a basket around, and each of us dropped a kernel of dried corn into the basket. The kernel of dried corn was accompanied by a brief offering of thanks to the Lord. I was a sophomore in college and a bit too spiritual for my own good. I composed my remarks carefully so that God would be pleased and my family would be impressed, but my grandmother spoke spontaneously from her heart. Her eyes filled with tears that year as she spoke from her place at the far end of a long life. She confessed that she and my grandfather were naïve and inexperienced in the ways of God and life when they first started out. She ended by commenting that she could never have imagined at the beginning the blessings God had in store for them. She looked around the table at each of us, her gaze lingering the longest on my grandfather's face.

My grandmother's perspective was one I could not understand as a nineteen-year-old. I was barely an adult and did not have a

137

personal history to speak of. My life was a pinpoint. By comparison hers was a long line. In many ways I resembled God's early family members in Genesis. I was an infant. Just as an infant interprets life merely by observing the near and the here and now, my view of life was limited to the little that I knew.

Within six months of that Thanksgiving meal, my grandfather was dead of a sudden heart attack. My grandmother later confided to me that she intuitively felt on that Thanksgiving afternoon around the oversized table, that she and my grandfather were celebrating their last Thanksgiving together on earth. Her expression of gratitude, poured out for all of us to hear, was a mournful swan song at the end of life full of beautiful music. I'm not as old as my grandmother was then, but I am much older than I was. Like her, I can look back over phases and periods of my life and be thankful God has made himself known in each.

QUESTIONS FOR REFLECTION

1. How does viewing your own life from a time line or wider lens perspective help you?
2. What does such a view teach you about God?
3. Where would you place yourself on the time line of God's children throughout Scripture?
4. Where would you place your children?
5. What would it take to mature to the next level?

If

If I look on ones I love and see them rejecting truth, the truth
of heaven and the exclusive right of Jesus alone to transport them
there, the truth that Scripture dictates right and wrong about their
morality, relationships, sexuality. And if I watch in grief and horror
as my loved ones act upon that rejection of truth in their beliefs and
their behavior, oh, how sweet an escape it would be to abandon my
grief and horror by simply altering what I believe. If I choose to
ignore the truths my loved ones have broken themselves upon, I can
avoid such agony. Rather than face my pain in its fullness, I can
lessen or obliterate it if I choose to believe God says less than he
really does.

I will appear more compassionate, more tolerant, when in
reality I am adopting a view that . . .

Is a result of emotional cowardice. I have neatly sidestepped a
chasm of suffering. I now need not weep over an erring friend.
I need not agonize in prayer. I have reasoned away such invest-
ments in them and made my love so much easier.

Asserts myself as more compassionate than God himself. I am,
in essence, redefining him and his attributes. I am replacing the
consuming fire with the soft glow of benign tolerance.

Refuses to identify with the cross. I am looking on Jesus, the
Suffering Servant, and saying to his bloodstained face, "I choose not
to love as you do. Your love sweats drops of blood, and that I cannot do. I will look on both thieves on the cross and casually include
them in your kingdom; it is easier that way. Their rejection cannot
hurt me this way."

And if I choose this wide way, limiting my faith to that which
makes love easy, may a more noble soul ache over me in prayer and
grieve over me in love.

CHAPTER TWENTY-FIVE
Magic-Wand Theology

W hen I was younger, I believed in the magic wand theology of healing. Just go to Doctor God with your boo-boo and *poof* the hurt would instantaneously disappear. I honestly believed that whenever I discovered a wound—either self-inflicted or otherwise— in my own heart, a quick trip to the gates of heaven would heal the wound. My own experience was not always consistent with this dogma, but I believed it nonetheless. But theology is not reserved for spheres of scholarly speculation only. Our theology affects our here and now. Belief in a God of the cheap cure made me impatient with myself and with others. I wrongly assumed that a hurtful habit, an inner wound, a crooked way of thinking could be marched down the aisle to the altar and zapped into wholeness. This belief also implied that if the hurt persisted, I had somehow done something wrong.

Time, trouble, and teenagers have taken me to the deeper recesses of Scripture where I have discovered that healing *usually* involves a process. Psalm 147:3 says, "He heals the brokenhearted and binds up their wounds" (NIV). The psalmist uses an image with which we are all familiar. Bandages are used to cover a healing wound, to keep the medicine fresh and the pollutants away, and are replaced with new ones again and again until the wound is healed. It is a process that takes place over time. My brother-in-law still remembers the bandages the doctor applied to his back over and over again when he was a small boy. He had fallen while walking down an escalator, and his clothing and his back caught in the teethlike metal steps as they disappeared into the floor. One day I happened upon the rather gruesome pictures of his back taken by the insurance company not long after the accident. The nature of the gear-like gouges on his back clearly demanded the tedious process of bandaging. What my brother-in-law remembers most are the trips to the doctor to have bandages that stuck to his back peeled away, taking layers of skin with them. Then fresh, clean ones would give him a short-lived relief. He had to endure those excruciating visits every day for weeks. My mother-in-law grimaces and can barely talk about the ordeal even fifty years later.

Pat Answers

As mothers and fathers, it is only natural that we would want to circumvent the healing process in our children, especially if it is slow and painful. We either want to fix the problem or fix them. Paul Bellheimer wrote a book whose title, *Don't Waste Your Sorrows*, has become a personal motto. I love the sense of spiritual efficiency it conveys. Because I've wasted some of my own sorrows, I don't want my children to make the same mistakes. So I instruct them every chance I get to look for the lessons in their experiences. This is really not such a bad idea, except that I often rush them quickly from "see the lesson" to "learn the lesson" as if each function were one and the same. Not so. The learning is a process. And just because I can clearly see the lesson in an experience doesn't always mean I am healed by that lesson.

One rainy Saturday morning our son Stephen and I were driving home from his appointment to have an MRI. Indoor soccer that winter had been a fun diversion, but the torn cartilage in his left knee had left him unable to run track or play club soccer that spring. Stephen has been known to refer to the soccer field as paradise. He usually plays soccer for both school and a club league simultaneously and, when he isn't at practice, imposes a regimen of drills and conditioning on himself at home. (I think a microscopic view of his blood cells might reveal black-and-white octagons swimming around on the glass slide.) This MRI and the surgery that was sure to follow had ruined his day, to say the least. Ever the dispenser of pat answers, I soothed him on our dreary drive home with, "You know, Stephen, sometimes God uses physical problems over which we have no control to remind us that he is in control and we are not."

Stephen: "Mom, I *know* God is in control. I just want to play soccer!"

Mom—sheepish silence.

Stephen—frustrated silence.

Do I Only See a Lesson?

Jesus' disciples were often impatient for pat answers as well. John 9 tells us Jesus was "passing by" and saw "a man blind from birth." Reduce verse 1 to its core, and you have this: "Jesus saw a man."

The disciples, on the other hand, saw a problem, a question, a lesson, if you will. My sister Beth is well acquainted with what it feels like to be a lesson. She has cerebral palsy and endured quite a few surgeries in her childhood. Because the hospital where most of these occurred was a teaching hospital, the rounds every morning to her bedside usually involved the surgeon plus an entourage of residents and students. Many years later the emotional scars from those early morning encounters can ache more than the physical scars she bears. Rarely was she addressed as a person. Not once was she asked, "How are you feeling?" or "How did you sleep?" Rarely did anyone make eye contact with her. Once her incision was examined, the experts would often remain in the room, leaning against the bedrails, with their backs to her, continuing their discussion about her in the third person. Although she couldn't go anywhere, she had the distinct impression that she was summarily dismissed. She was a syndrome, a disease, a case.

I wonder if that's how the blind man in John 9 felt when the disciples brushed him aside and asked Jesus, "Teacher . . . why was this man born blind? Was it a result of his own sins or those of his parents?" (v. 1 NLT). They ignored the man himself in their quest for the lesson his plight could teach them.

The Process of Healing

Jesus answered his disciples in one verse. The rest of the chapter is devoted to the blind man himself. It is interesting to note that this is one healing which Jesus performed slowly and methodically. Rather than speak a word and effect instant healing, he made a paste of mud and saliva, smoothed the mud over the man's eyes, and instructed him to "Go and wash in the pool of Siloam" (v. 7 NLT). The man did as he was told "and came back seeing!" (v. 7 NLT). Not only did his healing involve a process; it included a follow-up visit. In verses 35 through 38, Jesus finds the man in order to ensure that his spiritual blindness is healed as well. Their interaction ends with much more than the physical healing of the man's eyes. We know the healing process went deep because the last we hear from the blind man is this exclamation: "Yes, Lord," the man said, "I believe!" And he worshiped Jesus (v. 38 NLT).

When Jesus answered the disciples' questions about the blind man, he did not deny that there was a lesson to be learned, but he directed their attention away from the lesson itself to the Lesson Giver. His desire was to reveal himself, his power and person, in the man. The same is true for us and for our children. If that takes a long, arduous process to do it best, then so be it. We chafe at that. We want God to be reflected in our strengths and accomplishments. Or at least we want him to be honored by a swift resolution to all of our difficulties. We want others to be wowed by the miraculous conclusion to the hard chapters in our lives. We cannot imagine that God would show his power while taking his time. We find the redundancy of the lessons irksome.

My conversation with our son Stephen is evidence that I still want pat answers, easily digestible truth, and quick cures. I have learned to thank God for those when I get them, but not to expect them. God's healing of my own heart has been an ongoing process. It has taken time and involved methodical instruction. It has been slow going, but it has also given me hours upon hours in which I wait for Jesus, more keenly aware of just how blind, ill, or lame I am as I wait. Day after day he has singled me out for his healing touch. Year after year he has met me right in the middle of pain only to bring about a release that is all the sweeter for the wait. And, because these things have taken time, I have been able to do the very thing he loves so much: worship him and proclaim, "Yes, Lord, I believe!"

QUESTIONS FOR REFLECTION

1. How does your belief about the way God heals us affect your everyday life?
2. How have you discovered the healing of your heart to be a process?
3. Where are you in that process?
4. If you are not yet able to fully believe God or worship him, how can you begin to pray to that end?

CHAPTER TWENTY-SIX

Just Imagine

Whenever my husband gets on a plane, why do I picture the crash chronicled on the six o'clock news? I am what most would consider a positive person. (A friend suggested I title this book *The Perky Person's Approach to Pain*.) But, when it comes to the well-being of my family, my imagination can suffer from a pessimism that quickly gives birth to full-blown worry. An innocuous trip to the lake calls up visions of drownings and skiing accidents. I'm ashamed to admit that more than once I checked to make sure our firstborn was breathing. I'm hardly aware the images are there, but they are. I talk with mothers and discover that their minds play the same tapes. At least I am in good company.

If faith, in part, is imagination, then these flashes of disaster that play across the screen of my mind can erode my faith. And an actual calamity can evoke a dread that threatens to demolish my belief that God will win the day in my child's life. One day as I prayed for one of our sons, I tried to imagine the answer to my prayers. I pictured his face and could not see the answer there where it belonged. I saw only the current trend of stubbornness. I tried to envision the problem lifted and the perspective changed, but I couldn't. I was stuck with a picture that either stayed the same or worsened. I had entertained negative newsreels so for so long, my faith that the channel would change was gone.

Lost Faith

Perhaps the most tragic result of struggling through a crisis with your child is that your faith may be lost in the battle. Maybe your faith hasn't totally evaporated, but you are running on fumes. You may be like the father in Mark 9 who brought his son to some of the disciples for help. Peter, James, and John were away having a mountaintop experience with Jesus. The son's life had been plagued with epileptic-like attacks for as long as the father could remember. This despairing dad's plea to Jesus is one of the more familiar phrases in Scripture because there is not a believer on earth who can't relate to, "I believe. Help my unbelief" (Mark 9:24 HCSB).

Before even attending to the man and his son, Jesus addresses his own followers and says, "You faithless people. How long must I be with you until you believe?" (v. 19 NLT). His chagrin is obvious; he wants us to believe, and we don't. Jesus' response neither ignores the sad truth about us nor crushes us under a load of disappointment and condemnation. He is not disillusioned with us because he has no illusions about us! His statement has the ring of a direct diagnosis. It is an uncomfortable but straightforward fact that our faith is lacking. Even those who have developed giant faith over the years can feel the truth of this assessment. Compared to what Jesus is capable of doing, our belief that he can do it is slim, especially when we despair over our children.

After dealing with his disciples, Jesus turns to the father. We don't have to look closely to hear the hurt and hopelessness this father must have felt. "Do something, if you can, take pity on us and help us!" (v. 22, author's paraphrase). Jesus notices that telling *if*. I love his gentle rebuke of this hurting father. Although he seems offended, he says something that must have made that doubting dad's heart sing, "Everything is possible to the one who believes" (v. 23 HCSB). Jesus exposes the possibilities—everything! And then he actually does the "everything" most desired by that family: he heals the son.

What are you imagining for your child's life that erodes your ability to have faith? How have you said to God, "If you can," with heavy emphasis on the *if*? Do you find yourself lamenting that "the only thing left to do is pray," as if jumping off a cliff would be just as effective? Do your prayers amount to not much more than worrying and fretting out loud? Does your son leave the house with your fears and panicked pictures trailing behind him? Does your daughter carry your distrust of God's protection on her dates? Do you find yourself wincing at God's promises rather than welcoming them? There is a good, old-fashioned, biblical word for that kind of thinking: it is called doubt. The father's faith was tainted with doubt that expressed itself in what he thought and said. It crept into his day-dreams. It robbed him of joy and anticipation just as it does us.

Faith Lessons

Where can we go when doubt defines us as parents? I think Jesus gave his disciples the beginning of an answer when he scolded them, "How long must I be with you until you believe?" (v. 19 NLT). *Being with Jesus* will eventually bring about faith. Being with any other in any other place has the potential to lessen my faith. *Being with Jesus* can change my imagination. Perhaps it can be stated as this simple formula: More Jesus = More Faith. Or a cry less formulaic: "Jesus, please *be with me* until I believe!" It is not unlike the cry of a child who needs the comforting presence of her mother in the dark, scary moments before sleep.

If faith is a gift from God (Eph. 2:8–9), then it stands to reason that time spent with the Gift-Giver will enrich the gift. In fact, time spent with Jesus may serve as the magnetic pull my heart needs to attract my gaze from his hand to his face. Gradually I am enthralled with *him*, not with the answer. So not only is my faith bolstered; it is redirected to the right place. I spent a good bit of the final months of my pregnancy with our first son flat on my back either at home or in a hospital bed. My first pregnancy had ended in miscarriage, and now this time, with just a few months to go, I was facing another heartbreaking end. I remember begging God for a healthy, full-term baby. And I remember his thoughts to me. He said something like this, "I love you, and I want to hear your requests. But your feet must rest on firm ground. A healthy baby is not something I have prom-ised you. My sufficiency for your every need is steady ground. Pray from there." Part of faith is believing that the ever-present help of a sovereign God will show up when I need it most. It is trusting that I will survive the days ahead in his "everlasting arms."

Another faith builder comes by the simple exercise of the minis-cule faith I *do* have. The father's "do something!" may have been uttered as a squeak, but it *was* uttered. It is easy to allow our grow-ing sense of failure as a parent, coupled with growing doubt, to keep us from boldly approaching the throne of grace with the shreds of faith that remain. It may take our last piece of strength to sink to our knees and send our tears heavenward, but sink we must. It is clear in this passage that a shred of faith is enough to move the hand of a healing, powerful God.

Finally, desperate times call for desperate measures. And the crash and burn of our pride as parents can be a monolithic measure for some of us. When the father said, "Help my unbelief," he admitted his neediness. He effectively confessed his sin. I wonder if Jesus' heart wasn't melted into even more compassion at those words. Here was a father who wasn't strong enough, secure enough, or spiritually stable enough to help his son. Just the humble state that allows for God's intervention.

Recently I spent some time with the Lord agonizing over an encounter with another of our sons. Nothing major, just a parent-teenager face-off that ended poorly. Once again I saw a bleak picture ahead and simply could not envision the flash point I knew needed to come in his life. Teenagers can be the epitome of pride, and a humble repentance was needed to resolve the issue. (Of course I needed a flash point of my own, but that's another chapter.) I could not imagine a resolution. I told God so. I sat longer with him, and he pulled back the curtain of my doubt. I saw it. In that moment I was able to alter my prayer from, "do something, if you can" to "do something, *you can*." I am certain that the eradication of my doubtful *if* was purely a function of *being with Jesus*.

I'm thankful for the inclusion in God's Word of this story. There is a parent who isn't perfect, a child with a need beyond the parent's powers, and a Savior who spells out some simple faith lessons I can use:

Be with Jesus.
Exercise whatever faith I have, however small.
Admit my need.
Begin to imagine what God can do.

Look back at that promise Jesus makes for a moment: "Everything is possible." Surely that encompasses the prayers we pray for our sons and daughters. Surely there is nothing I can imagine that steps outside the boundaries of "everything!" The path back to faith is paved with pictures of the everythings God can do. I may not see them yet, but I can begin to imagine them again.

QUESTIONS FOR REFLECTION

1. What are some of the fretful, negative newsreels about your family or one of your children in particular that play in your mind?
2. How do those thoughts affect your words, your actions, your faith?
3. What are some of the dreams and hopes you have for your children?
4. How can you incorporate those hopes into your daily prayer life? How can you make strides toward believing God for those prayers?
5. Finally, what step can you take toward being with Jesus in order to bolster your hopes?

CHAPTER TWENTY-SEVEN

Do I Have
What It Takes?

"I have never been more exhausted in all my life," our sweet friend Laura sighed. Had she just run the Boston Marathon or stayed up all night studying for an exam? No, she had spent her weekend watching our kids! Mind you, my husband and I were speaking at a retreat and actually had the kids (just two of the more to come) in tow. I still nursed the baby, watched both children during break times, sat with them at meals, and kept them in the room with us at night. Laura was along to entertain and watch them during the speaking sessions. I called her at noon on Monday to thank her, only to find her sacked out and thoroughly spent.

Laura is a hardy soul; in fact she now has children of her own, works hard, and has proved her mettle. But parenting at any stage is just plain hard work. When the kids are little, it is physically exhausting; and as they grow, it becomes emotionally and mentally exhausting. It is easy to feel like an air traffic controller watching radar blips dance on a screen, except that there are more blips than it is humanly possible to watch. Add to those dancing radar blips the glare of a crash or two, and the strain can be unbearable.

One day my journal read, "I am just not up to it today. I can't do it. I feel like an unloaded gun, a dry paintbrush, an injured athlete about to enter the game, an empty water bottle in the hands of a thirsty runner, like I don't have what it takes, like I've bitten off more than I can chew, and I'm choking." I was tempted to leave the couch, having expressed my malaise on paper, to grimly face the day, but the inertia born of a sense of defeat kept me there. I listlessly opened my Bible to Matthew 14. As I read the all-too-familiar story of Jesus feeding the five thousand, a striking solution came to my rescue. It went something like this: Jesus + A Few Loaves and Fish = More Than Enough. Therefore, Jesus + My Total Lack of Ability and Energy = More Than Enough. If ever there was a real panacea for parents—at any stage, in any circumstances, in any condition—this is it. Simplistic? Yes. True? Yes.

Resources . . . Without Fail

In the book of Ezra, God's people, led by Ezra, set out to rebuild the temple. It is amazing to read the political, cultural, and social hurdles they had to cross to do so. It is a wonder they didn't give up. But one thing stands out: through two different kings God provided all the resources they needed for the job. At the outset King Cyrus decreed, "The expenses of these men are to be fully paid . . . so that the work will not stop. Whatever is needed . . . must be given them daily without fail, so that they may offer sacrifices pleasing to the God of heaven" (Ezra 6:8–10 NIV). Fast-forward past some pretty obnoxious opposition to this proclamation by the next king, "Now I, King Artaxerxes, order all the treasurers of Trans-Euphrates to provide with diligence whatever Ezra the priest, a teacher of the Law of the God of heaven, may ask of you" (Ezra 7:21 NIV).

These are real kings, in real moments of history, giving real resources to a real, very needy people. The adverbs are stunning: their needs "are to be *fully* paid," provided "*with diligence*," given "*without fail*." To what purpose? "So that they may offer sacrifices pleasing to the God of heaven." This paradox could not be more suited to parenting. God's people were given resources in order to have enough to sacrifice. God fills us so that we may pour it back out. One of the most irksome yet noble aspects of raising children is the element of sacrifice. It is not a natural function, at least not wholehearted, pure sacrifice. By its very nature, sacrifice depletes us. We would not be able to do it, if not for adequate provision.

How Much Is Enough?

The first chapter of Ephesians echoes the kind of lavish provision made for God's people in Ezra. This list defines the "enough" we need. Here is a list from verses 3 through 11 (NLT) of what we get when we are on God's dole:

1. "Every spiritual blessing in the heavenly realms" (v. 3 NLT). Whoa! The list could stop right there, and we would have enough.
2. Adoption as children (v. 5).
3. His kindness—not meted out but "poured out" (v. 6).
4. Forgiveness—not grudgingly offered but "showered" on us (v. 7).
5. A lavish outpouring of his grace (v. 8).
6. Revelation to us of his "secret plan" (v. 9).
7. An inheritance from God himself (v. 10).

Notice the currency of this list. There are no promises of enough physical prowess, enough skill, enough excess funds to pad our accounts, but we often believe that is the legal tender we need to succeed, even as parents. One summer I became convinced I was failing as a parent because we didn't have the financial resources that year for camps and swim clubs. Neither did we have the money to buy a modicum of coolness for our boy's wardrobes, and they were starting to notice. In a world that values constant activity and current fashion, I lamented that we didn't have the resources to raise our kids adequately. I was wrong. Our goal is not to raise busy, cool sons. If our goal is to raise godly young men, what we *need* is heaven. And heaven's reservoir is wide open to us. Read on in Ephesians, and the list of spiritual provisions expands to overflowing proportions.

Now back to those loaves and fish. We've relegated that story to the children's books; perhaps the simplicity of its message offends us. Perhaps we would rather take note of what we *don't* have. A child may sing, "Give me oil in my lamp, keep me burning, burning, burning. Give me oil in my lamp I pray. Hallelujah!" while a grown-up parent speaks of burnout. Have you spent most of your time lately focusing on what you don't have rather than the resources you do have? At the end of a particularly grueling day, one in which my reservoir is left dry, it is hard to believe the truth of Ephesians 1. Read that list again. That is hardly spiritual fumes; it catalogs the ingredients in a rich fuel designed to power a life of God-pleasing sacrifice. And this spiritual energy, if you will, has already been deposited in my tank.

Just Ask

My grandmother owned a farm in the flatland of west Texas. I remember overhearing speculation about oil on that land. I know there was a time when efforts were made to tap into whatever oil might be deep in the ground. I vaguely remember talk of money, time, effort, and displaced crops. Drilling for oil was not a cheap venture. I am aghast these days when I look at the price on the neon gas station signs. I've never had a clerk chirp out to me over his intercom, "Welcome to the black Jeep! Just pop off your gas cap, and we'll top off your tank with our highest-grade fuel! In fact, bring over a few gas cans for us to fill to the brim. It's all on us!" The provision God offers is not unearthed by our tools or bankrolled from our accounts. If not, how do we access it? How do I, at the end of a particularly grueling, depleting day, call up what I need from him?

Could it be as simple as asking? The treasurers of Ezra's day were instructed to dole out provisions "with diligence" based on whatever "he may ask." He simply had to ask. Most of us are not comfortable asking. For anything. If asking was discouraged or even punished in the homes we grew up in, we may even have a pathological aversion to it. Or we may be so enamored with our own independence that we will press on without ever thinking to ask. Many of us associate asking with shame. And others simply feel asking isn't proper or polite.

I remember running a 10k race with a friend. Neither of us were runners. The race took place in July, and as the day got steamier and steamier, the last long hill swam before us as more challenging than a climb up Kilimanjaro. All along our route spectators had cheered us on. By the time we rounded that last bend, I'm sure they were weary too since we were among the last to drag over the finish line. But those fans were our lifeline. I get embarrassed thinking about it, but my friend and I actually solicited support from the cordoned-off audience. If they didn't roar, we couldn't run. So, in our desperation to finish strong, we limped past, waving for encouragement. Physically we were "at the end of ourselves" and therefore shameless.

Maybe that's what it takes to get us to ask for the "more than enough" we need to kick in. Maybe the bewilderment we feel as parents can be viewed as a priceless blessing for this reason alone: we are driven to *ask*; we might not otherwise. The kind of asking that seeps out of our souls when we are empty is more akin to beseeching or begging than it is to requiring or demanding. In his 1828 *American Dictionary of the English Language*, Noah Webster points out that to ask is not to demand or require, which "imply a right or supposed right in the person asking." Ask is more linked to "beseech," which "implies more urgency, than ask. Ask and request imply no right, but suppose the thing desired to be a favor." Call it what you will, asking is a simple, childlike task few of us venture to undertake. In her book of poems, *Sitting by My Laughing Fire*, Ruth Bell Graham ponders our foolish disinclination to ask.

> *O tenderest Love,*
> *how we do fail*
> *through our own folly*
> *to avail*
> *ourselves of You.*
> *Cold,*
> *we shun*
> *Your warmth,*
> *Your sun;*
> *dry,*
> *Your dew,*
> *Your everflowing Spring;*
> *and pressured much,*
> *we miss Your gentle,*
> *calming touch;*
> *then wonder, "Why?"*
> *O pitying Heart,*
> *forgive*
> *the pauper spirit*
> *that would live*
> *a beggar*
> *at Your Open Gate*
> *until it is too late*
> *—too late.*[10]

There is a two-verse story in the book of Joshua that illustrates beautifully the "open gate" aspect of God's heart when we simply ask. For several chapters we read about the allotment of real estate in the promised land to each of the tribes of Israel. No one is left out. In Joshua 15 we find this interchange between Caleb and his newly married daughter Othniel. At her husband's urging, she has already secured a field. In verse 18, she alights from her donkey, and before she can form the question, Caleb asks her, "What can I do for you?" (NIV).

"She replied, 'Do me a special favor. Since you have given me the land in the Negev, give me also springs of water'" (NIV). I am tempted to think Othniel is being selfish until I picture my own dad. He has, in effect, asked me, "What can I do for you?" many times. And he delights in fulfilling my answers.

Caleb is no different from most other dads. Verse 19 tells us he not only gave her a spring; he gave her two of them, "the upper and lower springs" (NIV). When I consider that we have a Father and King who is standing in the wings of our lives asking, "What can I do for you?" I can't help but wonder that we stubbornly refuse to ask and, in failing to do so, miss the comforts of heaven. As parents, we would do well to simply ask before it is too late—too late.

QUESTIONS FOR REFLECTION

1. How have you spent most of your time lately focusing on what you *don't* have rather than what you *do* have?
2. What sacrifices must you make as a parent that require more of you than you can give?
3. How can you tap into the resources that have been provided for you?
4. Why is it so difficult to ask?

CHAPTER TWENTY-EIGHT
Fifth Graders and Healing

I have always loved fun. In fact, in my younger years I could have called it my "profession." I can't remember *ever* studying on the weekends in college; there was not room in my packed schedule of fun. I'm usually the self-appointed cruise director at any gathering, the one who feels personally responsible if we don't all have fun. For me, one symptom of just how deeply I felt our family's hurt was the total eradication of my fun capacity. This, of course, is hindsight; I was too immersed in grief at the time to notice.

So when it came time for me to chaperone my son's fifth-grade trip, I saw it as a task to be endured. In fact, because of the amount of energy it would require, this particular outing scored a high "dread factor" (a scale we sometimes use at our house). But the week before the trip, I made a pivotal choice. In the spirit of Colossians 3:23, "Whatever you do, do it enthusiastically, as something done for the Lord" (HCSB), I determined to chaperone wholeheartedly. I had to be there anyway, so I might as well. I would hike, play, interact, learn (which involved swamps and snakes) with all my heart. I would leave my hurt behind and "be there" for my son and his fifth-grade buddies. I didn't *feel* like it, but I would dive right in.

Well, when God wants to heal you, beware the medicine. We ran, canoed, laughed, built a bonfire, all with a childlike gusto I had forgotten I had, and presto chango, those wild and woolly fifth-graders restored my fun capacity! When I returned, the hurt was still at home and still within me. But fun with sixty plus fifth-graders redeemed my hope in the promise of better days. Playing hard with kids whose love for life and anyone who will play with them exercised my ability to "rise above" it all, even if only for a brief few days.

Rediscovering Hope

I remember those few days with a fondness that is far deeper than fifth-grade fun. Does that mean I was so shallow or immature that I could not find hope in prayer or in God's Word? Sheepishly, I have to admit that that is partially so, though I *did* find hope in those places. But I also believe God dished it out to me *everywhere*. How kind of him to show it to me cognitively *and* intuitively. I read, "Weeping may remain for a night, but rejoicing comes in the morning" (Ps. 30:5 NIV), knowing it to be fact. But facts don't always bathe the soul. Laughing out loud, discovering a crocus hiding beneath last fall's dead leaves, smelling the warm brownies a neighbor delivers: these enliven the fact of hope. *Fun* can restore.

When you had your first child, either watched or lived the intense miracle of birth, wasn't your heart full of hope? That hope helps make us effective as parents. We discipline, read to, teach, instruct, and discuss with a hope for a certain outcome. We don't potty train our two-year-olds with hopes that they will still be in diapers when they trot off to college. We act out an agenda with an end in sight. We poise on our knees beckoning our child to take those first tentative steps toward us and know that it won't be long until we're chasing a running toddler everywhere. We call out spelling words with a hope for at least a decent grade on the Friday test. The milestones our children pass are difficult enough: if we didn't coach them through them, *hopefully* they would become much more difficult tasks. We don't envision something in order to make it so (to test *that* theory, try feeding beets to a finicky two-year-old), but our hoping for a certain outcome does create an environment most conducive to positive change.

> So stands the Thracian herdsman with his spear,
> Full in the gap, and hopes the hunted bear.
> —Dryden

As parents, we *hope* obedience, manners, kindness, and neatness for our children. We wield it as a verb alongside the more obvious actions of *teach* and *train*. Augustine saw hope this way: "Hope has two beautiful daughters. Their names are anger and courage; anger at the way things are and courage to see that they do not remain the way they are."

Hope: Lost and Found

That kind of hope can be lost. A hurting, hostile, errant young man or woman in our home can drive us toward hopelessness. Even the healthiest of teenagers can leave us thinking,

Where is all that stuff I taught him?
Last year she had the most basic lessons down pat, and now it
    has all atrophied!
Will things ever be right again?

Those thoughts can lodge and fester and breed a hopeless outlook. We become like young parents waiting for our toddler's first steps with our backs turned. We've lost hope, and we need it back.

Hope is closely akin to faith; therefore it is a gift. If I am Christ's and an heir to "every spiritual blessing in the heaven" (Eph. 1:3 HCSB), then hope is available to me. The condition of my family is not the condition for hope. So much of this book is about regaining hope. The Word of God speaks it loud and clear. But, again, God offers pictures of it everywhere. Emily Dickinson heard it in the birdsong outside her window: "Hope is the thing with feathers that perches in the soul."

Childlike Remedies

Jesus, knowing our grown-up tendency to lose hope, sat a child on his lap as a poignant picture of the kingdom: "Therefore, whoever humbles himself like this child—this one is the greatest in the kingdom of heaven" (Matt. 18:4 HCSB). One thing I love about children is their keen powers of observation. They notice the simplest things and delight in them. One of the sad facts of adolescence is that the childlike ability to enjoy an inchworm or the cloud patterns in the sky is lost. Adolescent pride forbids the blessed aha's and look at that's of childhood. It isn't cool to stand awed by the kaleidoscope foliage of fall or the blurred vermilion of a hummingbird's throat.

I know now that those fifth graders God sent to restore my hope were about to lose the precious commodity of wonder. I feel privileged to have been included in what may have been their swan song. By sixth grade most of them were too cool to play with such abandon. For them and for me the time was just right for an epiphany. As they were becoming more like my species, I became more like theirs!

It could have easily been otherwise. Too often my adulthood serves as a shield, protecting me from the whimsical visions of hope a younger look at life might bring. I have at times been so mired in sorrow that I missed the unlikely hand that promises to pull me out. In *The Lord of the Rings*, J. R. R. Tolkein's great epic tale of hobbits, elves, dwarves, and other creatures, the hobbits often represent a curious mixture the playfulness of children with the sagacity of elder statesmen. In *The Return of the King*, the hobbit Pippin is called upon by the seasoned warrior Denethor to serve the besieged soldiers of Gondor.

> *"Can you sing?"*
>
> *"Yes," said Pippin. "Well, yes, well enough for my own people. But we have no songs fit for great halls and evil times, lord. We seldom sing of anything more terrible than wind or rain. And most of my songs are about things that make us laugh; or about food and drink, of course."*
>
> *"And why should such songs be unfit for my halls, or for such hours as these? We who have lived long in the Shadow may surely listen to echoes from a land untroubled by it? Then we may feel that our vigil was not fruitless, though it may have been thankless."*

As parents of a hurting son or daughter, we certainly live "long in the Shadow" and, like weary soldiers, are in desperate need of a tune from "a land untroubled by it." Perhaps the moral here is to look for hope as a child would look for four-leaf clovers. Or be ready for it to catch you. And if it ambushes you, enjoy it. God's design is to offer it to us, even if it takes a cabin full of fifth-graders to deliver the message.

QUESTIONS FOR REFLECTION

1. Have you experienced anything lately, regardless of how seemingly insignificant, that reminds you to be hopeful? Describe that experience.
2. How does it give you hope that you will someday rejoice again?
3. As you observe young children, what qualities do they possess that you need to regain?
4. How can you reaffirm your hope in God's desire to redeem your children and your home?

CONCLUSION

The Mystery

Most of us love a good mystery now and then. Whether such novels are guilty pleasures for our beach vacations or a regular reading habit, we like them *because of the mystery*, not in spite of it. The puzzles in plot tantalize us. The ambiguous characters beguile us. The unnamed shadows cast on the stage draw our attention. What genre of fiction more closely mirrors real life than the mystery novel? And what aspect of real life is most mysterious? Parenting. Yet here is a vital difference: the reader of a good mystery novel may willingly suspend his sense of security for the momentary thrill of insecurity because of the certainty of a satisfactory conclusion in the final chapter. But in the dark and difficult mysteries of life (there are light, ecstatic mysteries as well), the present insecurities in the plot can seem unbearable. We cannot so easily thumb to the final chapter to preview the end.

Thus far I have written twenty-eight chapters about the mysteriously unfolding outcome of our most precious plotlines: our children. I have empathized with you in those corners where the darkness of your son or daughter's life has rendered your own life terribly mysterious. But unlike Erle Stanley Gardner, Arthur Conan Doyle, or, my favorite, Dorothy L. Sayers, none of us acts as an omniscient author, piloting the likes of Perry Mason or Hercule Poirot through a drama of our own invention. This is not predicable, tidy fiction. As parents, we play the role of reader and hardly ever pen the script. Or as one friend so aptly put it, "I wrote the script, and my kids don't follow it."

In case you cannot tell, this is the final chapter of a book about mystery. I wish I could write it like one. My human flesh desires to act as the wise untangler of the mysteries in your home. At best,

I can pay a visit to those standard journalistic questions: who, what, and when.

Who

The "who" in the struggle to find meaning in our mystery is really no mystery. While waiting for our childrens' final chapters, we who are living ours have clear instructions: "In all your ways acknowledge Him, and He will make your paths straight" (Prov. 3:6 NASB). One of the simple household chores which I perform once or twice a day without even thinking, is to stoop down, grasp the dhurrie runner in our downstairs hallway by the fringe, and gently snap the offending rumples out of it so that it is straight and flat again. The constant traffic of soccer cleats, tennis shoes, bare feet, dog paws, and occasional rolling objects cause the rug's design to wrinkle into crooked folds that make it neither attractive nor safe. By continually acknowledging the God who knows every errant fold in my path, the mysteries, I am connecting to the only One who can firmly grasp my path and snap it straight again.

What

The "what" our hearts ask is fairly straightforward as well. Most of us have been catapulted by pain far beyond the surface "whats" of our children's lives to the bottom line. I believe we all long for roughly the same version of the same final chapter. Third John 4 says, "I have no greater joy than this, to hear of my children walking in the truth" (NASB). In John 8:32 Jesus promises, "You shall know the truth, and the truth shall set you free" (NKJV). I often drink my morning coffee from a big black mug that bears the phrase in bold white letters: **Absolutely Free**. The mug was a gift from a drug rehab program where hundreds of teenagers have found freedom from drug addiction. That is a sweet freedom, I admit, but it is not *absolute* freedom. Freedom that is absolute is found only in the Truth.

When

The "when" question may be the most painful question we ask. It is perhaps the most mysterious. This question echoes hauntingly in the great chasm that seems to stretch from my today and the today yet to be found in the final chapter. I remember suffering with a splinter in my finger as a young child. I knew my dad would get out the Mercurochrome (the orange stuff that stings), sterilize a needle, and then . . . I couldn't bear to think of it. So I let the splinter fester and throb in my finger until someone noticed that I was in agony. The day or so of waiting seemed eternal, but the microsurgery my dad performed had a swift, sure moment of instant relief!

We cannot plot the final chapter of our child's true homecoming on our calendars, and it would be foolish and cruel to assert that the healing of broken relationships, drug abuse, or deep hurts could be scheduled in such a way. Neither can we believe that healing will always happen in the twinkling of an eye. But the walk into truth begins with an abrupt direction change. Luke 15 does not record how long the shepherd searched for the lost sheep, the precious one of the hundred in his flock. We are not told how long it took the frantic woman to find her missing silver coin. No one knows how much time elapsed before the prodigal son "came to his senses" and traveled home. His father was not even privy to that moment until the drastic change in direction brought him all the way to the edge of his dad's estate (we don't know how much time that trip took either). But however long the wait, we know that those who were once lost *became found* in an instant.

In a poignant worship chorus, the words, "Yesterday was the day that I was alone, now I'm in the presence of Almighty God," are a reminder that the darkest chapter may be the next to last! While our hope is grounded in the "who"—the Solver of all mysteries—this is balm for the soul: to know that, when the turning to Jesus comes, it comes in a moment. We know that the mystery-solving last chapter of salvation and redemption will signal, not an end, but a beginning.

Notes

1. C. S. Lewis, *George MacDonald: An Anthology* (New York: MacMillan Publishing Company, 1947), 144.

2. "I Like It, I Love It" Words and Music by Steve Dukes, Markus Anthony Hall and Jeb Anderson. Copyright © 1995 Dream Works Songs (ASCAP), EMI Full Keel Music (ASCAP), Lehsem Music, LLC (ASCAP) and Publishing Two's Music (ASCAP). Worldwide Rights for Dream Works Songs Administered by Cherry Lane Music Publishing Company, Inc. Rights for Lehsem Music, LLC and Publishing Two's Music Administered by Music & Media International, Inc. International Copyright Secured. All Rights Reserved.

3. C. S. Lewis, *That Hideous Strength* (New York: MacMillan Publishing Company, 1946), 229–30.

4. *Baker's Evangelistic Dictionary of Biblical Theology* (Grand Rapids, Mich.: Baker Book House, 1996), 22.

5. C. S. Lewis, *The Four Loves* (Orlando, Fla.: Harcourt and Brace, 1960), 121.

6. Francis Thompson, *The Hound of Heaven* (Wilton, Conn.: Morehouse-Barlow Company, 1947), 5–6, 26.

7. Rudyard Kipling, "We and They" from *Poems for a Good and Happy Life*, compiled by Myrna Reid Grant (Garden City, NY: CrossAmerica Books, 1997), 54.

8. Ross Campbell, *How to Really Love Your Child* (Wheaton, Ill., Victor Books, 1977), 120.

9. Sandra Anne Taylor, *Secrets of Attraction: The Universal Laws of Love, Sex and Romance* (Carlsbad, Cal.: Hay House, 2001).

10. Ruth Bell Graham, *Sitting by My Laughing Fire* (Waco, Tex.: Word Books, 1977).